D0220365

Food and Aviation in the Twentieth Century

Food in Modern History: Traditions and Innovations

Series Editors
Peter Scholliers
Amy Bentley

This new monograph series pays serious attention to food as a focal point in historical events from the late eighteenth century to the present day.

Employing the lens of technology broadly construed, the series highlights the nutritional, social, political, cultural, and economic transformations of food around the globe. It features new scholarship that considers ever-intensifying and accelerating tensions between tradition and innovation that characterize the modern era. The editors are particularly committed to publishing manuscripts featuring geographical areas currently under-represented in English-language academic publications, including the Global South, particularly Africa and Asia, as well as monographs featuring indigenous and under-represented groups, and non-Western societies.

Food and Aviation in the Twentieth Century

The Pan American Ideal

Bryce Evans

BLOOMSBURY ACADEMIC
LONDON • NEW YORK • OXFORD • NEW DELHI • SYDNEY

BLOOMSBURY ACADEMIC
Bloomsbury Publishing Plc
50 Bedford Square, London, WC1B 3DP, UK
1385 Broadway, New York, NY 10018, USA
29 Earlsfort Terrace, Dublin 2, Ireland

BLOOMSBURY, BLOOMSBURY ACADEMIC and the Diana logo are trademarks of
Bloomsbury Publishing Plc

First published in Great Britain 2021
Paperback edition published 2022

Copyright © Bryce Evans, 2022

Bryce Evans has asserted his right under the Copyright, Designs and Patents Act, 1988, to
be identified as Author of this work.

For legal purposes the Acknowledgements on p. ix constitute an extension
of this copyright page.

Cover image © CSA-Printstock/Getty

All rights reserved. No part of this publication may be reproduced or
transmitted in any form or by any means, electronic or mechanical,
including photocopying, recording, or any information storage or retrieval
system, without prior permission in writing from the publishers.

Bloomsbury Publishing Plc does not have any control over, or responsibility for, any
third-party websites referred to or in this book. All internet addresses given in this
book were correct at the time of going to press. The author and publisher regret any
inconvenience caused if addresses have changed or sites have ceased to exist, but can
accept no responsibility for any such changes.

A catalogue record for this book is available from the British Library.

Library of Congress Cataloging-in-Publication Data
Names: Evans, Bryce, author.
Title: Food and aviation in the twentieth century : the Pan American ideal / Bryce Evans.
Description: London ; New York : Bloomsbury Academic, [2021] |
Series: Food in modern history: traditions and innovations |
Includes bibliographicalreferences and index.
Identifiers: LCCN 2020033464 (print) | LCCN 2020033465 (ebook) |
ISBN 9781350098848 (HB) | ISBN 9781350202818 (paperback) |
ISBN 9781350098855 (ePDF) | ISBN 9781350098862 (ePub)
Subjects: LCSH: Airlines–Food service–History–20th century. |
Pan American World Airways, Inc.–History.
Classification: LCC TX946.5 .E93 2021 (print) | LCC TX946.5 (ebook) |
DDC647.9/639–dc23
LC record available at https://lccn.loc.gov/2020033464
LC ebook record available at https://lccn.loc.gov/2020033465

ISBN: HB: 978-1-3500-9884-8
PB: 978-1-3502-7947-6
ePDF: 978-1-3500-9885-5
ePub: 978-1-3500-9886-2

Series: Food in Modern History: Traditions and Innovations

Typeset by Newgen KnowledgeWorks Pvt. Ltd., Chennai, India
Printed and bound in Great Britain

To find out more about our authors and books visit www.bloomsbury.com
and sign up for our newsletters.

Dedicated to the flight attendants of Pan American World Airways, and to Alice

Note on Terminology: British English spelling conventions have been used throughout this book. 'Airplane', however, is used instead of 'Aeroplane' because this object is specifically discussed as an instrument of American modernity and therefore deserves its American English spelling.

Contents

Figures

Acknowledgements

I am indebted to the generous support offered by the following institutions: University of Miami Archives and Special Collections; Truman Presidential Library; Hoover Presidential Library; Science History Institute; The College of Surgeons, Philadelphia; Pan Am Historical Foundation; West Virginia University Regional and Archives Center; Pan Am Museum Foundation; World Wings International; Georgia State University Archives; Foynes Flying Boat and Maritime Museum; British Airways Heritage Centre; National Air and Space Museum Archives; Economic History Society.

And to the kindness of the following people: Abigail Lane, Gabriella Williams, Nicola Hellmann McFarland, Cristina Favretto, Jason Sylvestre, Edward Nolan, Helen Davey, John Morgan, Louis Berman, Winnifred Omodt, Cornelis Van Aalst, Rebecca Sprecher, Bronwen Roberts, Marlies Suter, Harry Frahm, Renata Van Kempema, George Banks, Dian Groh, Barbara Scharfstein, Shreya Sehgal, Sybile Holder, Margie Thompson, Donna Valdes, Debbi Fuller, Joan Nell Bernstein, Barrie Fewster, Peter Evans, Greta Evans, Philip Martin, Inez Amaral de Sampaio, Barry O'Kelly, Clay Gransden, John Grant, Sabine Merta, Ian Rasmussen, Ken Lownds, Tony Presland, Nadia Berenstein, Geoff Tansey, Brigit Ramsingh and Ros Evans. My sincere apologies if I have accidentally omitted mention of anyone else from the Pan Am 'family' who kindly assisted with this project.

Introduction

This book is about food and aviation. What may seem at first glance like a niche topic is in fact a universal one. Many people have sampled airline food, and many have derided it. But while most people recognize the role of air travel in 'making the world a smaller place', few stop to consider how the food in the plastic container on the tray table in front of them is symbolic of globalization. Global interconnectivity, or transnationalism, was one of the great distinguishing features of the twentieth century; it describes the collapsing of national boundaries and the enhanced frequency of exchange between peoples. The transit of food by air, and the eating of different cuisines while airborne, was – and remains – a potent symbol of this process and, in the pages that follow, its colourful history is outlined. Yet such a universal topic demands more than a general history, it requires an in-depth study.

Therefore, the subject of this case study is a company commonly regarded as the greatest airline in history and one symbolic of American global power in the twentieth century. 'Come fly with me, let's fly, let's fly away' crooned Frank Sinatra in the eponymous hymn to the early jet age; the lyrics that followed – 'if you can use some exotic booze, there's a bar in far Bombay' – summed up the foreign allure of food and drink by air. In 1958, when the song was released, the novelty and glamour of transoceanic air travel was attached to the journey as much as the destination itself and, if listeners at the time were asked to guess which airline Sinatra's words might best apply to, the most common answer would have been Pan American World Airways.

Established by Juan Terry Trippe, the son of a New York stockbroker, 'Pan Am' was operative between 1927 and 1991 and achieved the majority of 'firsts' in commercial aviation history. Using his political connections, Trippe took advantage of the stock market crash of 1929 to take over a struggling rival's Latin American routes; his company swiftly went on to become the global emblem of the 'golden age' of air travel and its famous blue globe logo, as is often remarked, became the second most recognizable American brand behind Coca Cola. Pan Am was neither the first commercial airline in the world nor the first to serve food: in the very earliest days of air travel, European air services outstripped their American equivalents. But Pan Am's twentieth-century lifespan encapsulated like no other the airline industry's inimitable 'golden age' and twentieth-century trajectory, its jet age ascent, flourishing, and subsequent saturation. And food service, as discussed in the pages that follow, was central to this story; it was something, to the chagrin of its rivals, that the company came to perfect. Pan Am's reputation for good food was an integral part of its romantic and raffish myth and ideal. From the humble beginnings of a three-engine Fokker F7 flying the ninety or so miles from Florida's Key West to Havana in one hour and twenty-five minutes in 1927, the company grew into the first airline to span the oceans and the first to fly around the world; as it did so, it established a reputation for gastronomic excellence and played a leading role in the evolution of what may be termed transnational cuisine.

Yet Pan Am is historically important not merely because it was the largest international air carrier of the twentieth century but also because it operated as the 'chosen instrument' of the US government over several decades, effectively an arm of state carrying out strategic services deemed 'politically impossible' for the US federal authority.[1] In the interwar years, when the company was making its name, aviation discourse and imagery was ubiquitous in America. Flight had become a metaphor for US supremacy, an international power symbolized by the enormous three-and-a-half-ton rotating globe that was the centrepiece of Pan Am's Dinner Key Terminal in Miami, Florida. The airplane promised a new type of imperium, one based on markets, commerce and culture rather than older forms of conquest and colonization.[2] American soft power, transmitted through popular culture in movies and music, also extended to food brands, cultures of consumption and food assistance. In 1939 Professor Herbert Bolton, an adviser to the State Department, instructed US officials gathered to discuss the propaganda potential of culture that 'a nation's culture comprises the whole body of its civilization, *its way of life*' – and a distinctly American way of life was, of course, its way of producing, distributing and consuming food.[3]

---

[1] Cited in Marylin Bender and Selig Altschul, *The Chosen Instrument: Pan Am, Juan Trippe, and the Rise and Fall of an American Entrepreneur* (New York: Simon and Schuster, 1982), 21.

[2] Jenifer Van Vleck, *Empire of the Air: Aviation and the American Ascendancy* (Cambridge, MA: Harvard University Press, 2013).

[3] Quoted in Justin Hart, *Empire of Ideas: The Origins of Public Diplomacy and the Transformation of US Foreign Policy* (Oxford: Oxford University Press, 2013), 27.

The spirit of the age was famously encapsulated in an article published two years later by the publisher Henry Luce, writing in his own *Life* magazine, who challenged his fellow citizens to construct the 'American Century'. Distinct from the tyranny of old European colonialism, Luce offered an ideal vision of a new American-led internationalism which would transmit democratic and cultural ideals via new technologies such as the airplane and the radio instead of physical conquest.[4] This goal was pursued by the US government from 1943 onwards through its 'Projecting America' campaign, which used the latest advertising methodologies to portray American abundance.[5] The Second World War would prove an enormous boon not only to this goal but also to Pan Am's growth as it operated an enormous number of services for the US Army and Navy during the conflict.[6] Post-war, the globalizing ambitions of America, the great nation of nations, were accompanied by the sort of universalism Luce imagined and Pan Am – its prefix suggesting a homogenizing inclusivity – embodied this pan American ideal. It was therefore much more than an airline, it symbolized progress in the Americas and beyond: the New World transporting a new form of civilization to the Old. After the war, the company's monopoly on international flights was eroded, yet well into the 1970s Pan Am remained the unofficial overseas flag carrier of the United States. Its story is therefore also the story of American twentieth-century expansionism in times of both war and peace. As this study shows, the airline's association with food went beyond in-flight service as the company – showcasing Brand America – spearheaded US government programs delivering food security and food aid. In short, it was integral to the 'American Century' and the expansionist pan Americanism which distinguished it.

Pan Am's size, style, technological prowess and global reach ensured it continued to occupy iconic status. The commissioning of the *Pan Am* television drama series in 2011 hinted at the abiding appeal of its service. The serving of food and drink featured continuously in the programme, illustrating the fact that the company distinguished itself through this function, for Pan Am not only led the world in technological innovation but also set the standard for airborne food service, shaping the in-flight experience of food to this day. As is revealed in the pages that follow, this gourmet glamour was underpinned by both serious

---

[4] Henry Luce, 'The American Century', *Life Magazine*, 7 February 1941.
[5] Hart, *Empire of Ideas*, 88.
[6] See Report of the Civil Aeronautics Board to the Army and Navy on Pan American's Services and the flight personnel requirements and resources, Truman Library, George C. Neal papers, Pan American Airways file, box 26–9.

science and attention to the detail of fine dining culture from the Old World, all of which seems a far cry from the commonplace disdain of airplane food today. One food critic writes 'no airline meal can ever be good … it is cooked in an industrial kitchen … the chef is probably a dunderhead (few talented chefs opt for flight catering) … you'd be crazy to expect haute cuisine. If the food is anything more than disgusting, just be grateful.'[7] Why, then, do people pay to recreate the experience? Nostalgia for Pan Am's food service is now such that a Los Angeles film studio hosts a retro dinner on a stage set up to look like a double-decker Pan American Boeing 747 at which patrons, served by smiling young actresses dressed in Pan Am uniform, divest themselves of upwards of $200 each to dine 'airline'.[8] The answer, it is argued in the following chapters, lies with the brand, the people and the particular dynamics and geopolitics of the 'golden age' of air travel.

Airline food today continues to repel and fascinate. It is the subject of various online travelogues and blogs and there are even websites devoted to airline passengers' cell phone pictures of their in-flight meals.[9] That it is so clearly a subject of popular interest makes it all the more surprising that the subject lacks a rigorous academic study devoted to it.[10] In the only general study of the history of airline food, which is disappointingly short on primary sources, Pan Am is mentioned in passing but is not accorded the central role it deserves.[11] Meanwhile, memoirs by former airline catering personnel tend to include interesting reminiscence but lack detail.[12] The five main chapters of this study therefore seek to fill these gaps in knowledge. The first provides a narrative history of food and aviation focusing on the context in which Pan Am operated and outlining the technological advances that gave the company, and the United States, a competitive edge. The second chapter explores in greater depth the science underpinning the progress in airborne consumption in the twentieth century. The third chapter turns from the science to the cultural significance of

---

[7] Vir Sanghvi, *Rude Food: The Collected Food Writings* (New Delhi: Penguin, 2004), 161.

[8] See http://panamexperience.com/ (accessed 9 January 2017).

[9] See http://www.airlinemeals.net/ (accessed 9 January 2017).

[10] Richard Foss, *Food in the Air and Space: The Surprising History of Food and Drink in the Skies* (Langham, MD: Rowman and Littlefield, 2014). Foss provides an excellent introduction to the topic and his book is useful as a general text, but his archival source base is very limited, based only on primary sources from the British Royal Air Force Museum along with ephemera from Qantas. See also Philip J. Parrott, *The History of Inflight Food Service* (Houston: International Publishing Company of America, 1986).

[11] See George Banks, *Gourmet and Glamor in the Sky: A Life in Airline Catering* (London: GMS, 2006). This extensive and readable memoir on airline catering acknowledges Pan Am's lead role in its history.

[12] See, e.g., Helen McLaughlin, *Footsteps in the Sky: An Informal Review of U.S. Airlines Inflight Service 1920s to the Present* (Evanston, IL: State of the Art, 1994).

Pan Am's attempt to collapse the gastronomic borders separating the Old and New worlds. Next, the book addresses the most overlooked aspect of the history of airline food: the stories of those whose working lives revolved around it. The final chapter interrogates the broader geopolitical implications attached to the emergence of the transnational cuisine spearheaded by the great American carrier, revealing the paternalism masked by the pan American ideal.

In exploring the changing science and culture attached to food during Pan Am's global reign, this book provides the first serious academic study to highlight the company's gastronomic history and – through it – relay the story of food and aviation in the twentieth century: a story of US imperialism, the internationalization of markets and the emergence of transnational taste. In doing so it adds to the body of scholarship not only around food and travel but also around food as a domain of global studies. It thus builds on works which explore how food – as a social, cultural, political and economic commodity – has been used throughout history as an engine of expansion.[13] As a prime agent of US expansion and expansionism, Pan Am played a defining role in the construction of the 'American Century'. Hitherto overlooked in this process was the role of food and its unique food culture. Food was central to the company's unified luxury experience which placed both it and the United States at the forefront of modernity. However, as this book shows, this very same definition of modernity remained inherently elitist and imperialist. Pan Am, in pushing the pan American ideal, would simultaneously expose its flaws.

[13] See Sidney Mintz, *Sweetness and Power: The Place of Sugar in Modern History* (New York: Penguin, 1986); Raymond Grew, *Food in Global History* (Boulder, CO: Westview, 1999); Jeffrey Pilcher, *Food in World History* (New York: Routledge, 2006). Studies of the history of food and travel/transport/tourism include several studies by Jean Pierre Poulain, most notably 'S'adapter au monde ou l'adapter? L'alimentation en mouvement, des grandes migrations au tourisme', *Diasporas*, 7 – *Cuisines en Partage* (2005), 11–28; Poulain and Gabriel Larrose, *Traité d'ingénierie Hôtelière Conception et organisation des hôtels, restaurants et collectivités édition augmentée* (Paris: Editions Jacques Lanore, 1995); Philip McLaughlin, Laurence Tibère, 'Tourisme et altérité alimentaire', *Espaces* 202 (2003), 37–47. For work on food and railways see Jean-Pierre Williot, ed., *La restauration ferroviaire entre représentations et consommations* (Frankfurt: Peter Lang, 2017); and Francois Caron, 'Un chantier à ouvrir: l'histoire de la restauration à la SNCF. Premières orientations', *Revue d'histoire des chemins de fer* 41 (2010), 227–41; for food and cruise ships see Francois Desgrandchamps and Catherine Donzel, *Cuisine à bord: Les plus beaux voyages gastronomiques* (Paris: Editions de la Martinière, 2011).

1

From the Clipper to the 747: A narrative history of in-flight food from the 1920s to the 1980s

Food as entertainment: The role of the purser

In the 1920s flying was noisy, smelly and uncomfortable. The excessive vibration of the aircraft and the loud background noise accentuated the discomfort and anxiety felt by many passengers, emotions which, as a number of studies have shown, negatively impact taste perception.[1] One well-placed observer of flight food, to whom this book will regularly return, was Betty Trippe (née Stettinius), the sister of US Secretary of State Edward Stettinius Jr. and from 1928 the wife of Pan Am founder Juan Trippe. Betty's husband, Juan Trippe, was a Yale graduate and, as mentioned, came from a monied background himself, but in securing Betty as his spouse he had married very well indeed. Coming from the upper reaches of US high society, Betty was familiar with the culinary norms of the American wealthy. A frequent flier with Pan Am from its inception, her observations document the evolution of airline food service and convey how nerve-wracking those early flights were. On the inaugural 1929 Pan Am flight from Brownsville, Texas, to Mexico City, piloted by the renowned aviator Charles Lindbergh – the first man to fly across the Atlantic – Betty wrote about how the only food service was chewing gum passed around before take-off to prevent airsickness. The gum was accompanied by cotton buds for the ears and a brown paper bag for vomit. The flight itself was shaky, with passengers having to shout at one another to be heard. To cap it all, before landing a pungent-smelling insecticide was sprayed throughout the cabin, which resulted in coughing,

---

[1] These are summarized in Charles Spence, 'Tasting in the air: A review', *International Journal of Gastronomy and Food Science* 9 (2017), 10–15.

choking and streaming eyes.[2] In such circumstances it is hard to imagine anyone aboard settling down to enjoy an in-flight meal.

Indeed, the weight limits and general discomfort of the earliest air travel militated against the pleasant consumption of food. In 1920 the British company Daimler Airways was the first to employ a flight attendant to serve passengers from small folding tables, although his official title was 'cabin boy' and he served only light refreshments. While the British competed with the French to open the first 'flying restaurant', there is disagreement over whether it was Pan Am or the German carrier Lufthansa which offered the first *hot* meals in an airplane. Lufthansa can justifiably claim to have been the first airline that served food using culinary professionals (waiters), with meals kept hot by storage in thermos bottles.[3] As this suggests, the dining experience on airplanes proved less successful than that on the great airships of the early twentieth century which, although quickly overtaken by the airplane, afforded greater space and therefore greater possibilities when it came to food service, as outlined subsequently.

The early airlines quickly realized that food-based entertainment was a good way of distracting customers from the all-round unpleasantness of the flight experience. As the size of aircraft increased, so the possibilities for food service expanded accordingly. In particular, the early introduction of flying boats to Pan Am's fleet saw the company add a steward to the crew.[4] Pan Am's first steward, Amaury Sanchez, noted 'my only instructions were to keep people happy and not too scared'.[5] Naturally enough, a large part of this brief centred on food service. Due to the large number of layovers accompanying lengthy flights, passengers would usually eat breakfast and dinner at hotels on the ground. Lunch, however, was the responsibility of the head steward: the purser. A nautical term, the purser was traditionally the person in charge of handling money and other aspects of administration and provisioning on board ship. Back in the eighteenth and nineteenth centuries, the early air balloonists regarded themselves as 'mariners of the upper atmosphere'[6] and, to this day, air travel's embrace of the maritime persists – displayed most clearly in the standard navy-blue pilot's uniform. As this book shows, many of these norms derived from Juan Trippe and his embrace

---

[2] Betty Trippe, *The Diary and Letters of Betty Stettinius Trippe* (McLean, VA: Paladwr, 1982), 15.

[3] Foss, *Food in the Air and Space*, 20–4. The 'cabin boy' was chosen because he was lighter than an adult.

[4] Dian Stirn Groh and Becky Snider Sprecher, 'Dining Aloft', in Jeff Kriendler and James Patrick Baldwin (eds), *Pan Am – Personal Tributes to a Global Aviation Pioneer* (Miami: Pan Am Historical Foundation, 2017), 121–4.

[5] Amaury Sanchez, quoted in Phil Tiemeyer, *Plane Queer: Labor, Sexuality, and AIDS in the History of Male Flight Attendants* (Los Angeles: University of California Press, 2013), 20.

[6] See Richard Holmes, *Falling Upwards: How We Took to the Air* (New York: Random House, 2013).

of all things maritime. Trippe came from a family which had made its original wealth from the clipper sailing ships of the nineteenth century; accordingly, Pan Am adopted many terms from the seafaring world, including the term 'purser', which came to refer to the cabin manager aboard flights. As this move illustrates, as the airline business expanded the lone steward became a team of stewards, headed by the purser. During each day's flight, the purser would take orders from passengers before radioing ahead to have lunches and snacks prepared at fuelling stops.

In the early days of passenger flight, pursers would sometimes locally source the food served on the plane, buying items at markets if they were deemed safe to eat. Because there were no kitchens in early aircraft, meals would then be prepared in the kitchens of local hotels or at Pan Am's bases in locations such as Kingston, Jamaica. Once ready, the food would be boxed. The purser would collect the meals and serve them later, in the air, as box lunches.[7] According to one historian, these early in-flight meals resembled 'an ennobled flying picnic': the sandwiches and salads were served cold and the only warm item was the tea and coffee.[8] When it comes to Pan Am, however, the image of the flying picnic requires some revision, as the company's rapid expansion enabled its menus to develop apace. Between 1927 and 1941 Pan Am (through its subsidiary Panagra) enjoyed a virtual monopoly on all American flights to Mexico, the Caribbean islands and Central and Latin America, developing an extensive infrastructure of airfields, weather stations and radio navigation aids as it did so. The development of this infrastructure helped the company weather political change. After the Republican party was displaced by the Democrats in 1933 Pan Am continued to enjoy political favour, a period coinciding with the US's 'Good Neighbor' policy and deepening Latin American economic reliance on the United States.[9] In establishing US air dominance over the continent and keeping German competition down, the company was performing an important geopolitical role. In 1937, Asúncion (Paraguay) became the last of the twenty-one capitals south of the United States to be incorporated into Pan Am's system. It was therefore thanks to the variety of this first network of routes between the United States, the Caribbean and Latin America that an eclectic mix of cuisines

---

[7] Interview with Dian Groh, 12 January 2018.

[8] Guillaume de Syon, 'Airmeals: We are what we eat, but what happens when we fly?', *Sabor* 1 (2013), digital issue.

[9] See Juan Trippe's remarks on the political favour granted his airline by Presidents Coolidge, Hoover and Roosevelt in the statement of Juan Trippe before the President's Air Policy Commission, Washington, DC, 1 October 1947. Truman Library, Records of the president's Air Policy Commission, Pan American Airways System file, box 9.

and meal types was experienced by passengers, many inspired by the colonial history of the territories visited, and many of which were brought on board hot and consumed lukewarm. A company press release quoted a 'passenger' of the 1930s thus:

> Meals on this line are a regular kaleidoscope, the first lunch, at Cienfuegos, is Cuban. Then you get a French meal out of Port au Prince, Haiti. Next comes an American luncheon over San Juan, Puerto Rico. Then there is a good old British meal from St Johns, Antigua, British West Indies. Over Paramaribo, in Dutch Guiana, you get Dutch cooking, and over Cayenne, French Guiana, it's French again. Over Sao Luiz, Brazil, the meal is Portuguese, and over Caravellos, Brazil, it is German.[10]

The colonial character of these early food choices reflected two key points about early American in-flight dining: first, passengers were almost exclusively affluent and white; and second, acknowledging that it was catering to WASPish palettes, the company realized that 'native' fare was simultaneously titillating but not to be trusted. In constructing a menu with a frisson of exoticism yet anchored firmly in trusted Western culinary traditions, much depended on the individual flair of the purser. He was expected to possess some gourmet inspiration, heading for the local market after the plane landed and returning with local delicacies such as baby lobster or wild duck, which would be prepared in the hotel kitchens and presented both attractively and in a manner familiar to white North American passengers.

A certain degree of flamboyance and entertainment was duly expected of the purser, with passengers booking trips coinciding with their favourites being on board. Food, understandably enough, was central to the performance of what was, at heart, a role which took creativity and guile to carry off properly. It was a performance which, through food, transported passengers from Depression-era America to an alternative reality. It fell to the purser not only to order food and collect it from dockside or hotel but also to formulate and produce, using a typewriter, individual menus based on whatever foodstuffs he had been able to procure. The flying picnic, then, was rapidly becoming something much more substantial based upon mimicking aspects of fine dining rituals. If flying in the early days was only for the people who could afford it, reminiscent of their own 'ennobled' lifestyle, then the role that the purser occupied resembled nothing more closely than that of the butler of the big house. After service, he went

---

[10] 'From Venison-on-the-hoof to Pheasant-under-glass' (undated), University of Miami special collections, Pan Am collection no. 341, series I, box 292, folder 5.

from butler to member of the kitchen staff, reverting to the humbling status of dishwasher, cleaning the plates and, thanks to the low altitude of early flights, simply discarding any surplus food overboard.[11]

The 'Clipper': A design icon containing the first airplane galley

Although the role of the purser was becoming more important, technology dictated that airlines still prioritized offering passenger meals on the ground, even if they had the ability to serve them in the air. Plane technology before 1936 largely required land-based eating, and even after 1936 and the innovation of the first galleys on aircraft, eating on the ground was still considered preferable to in-flight dining. Flying long distances was very much a hop-on/hop-off experience and Pan Am's stopovers in different territories mirrored the less exotic model employed by US domestic carriers flying coast-to-coast. These airlines would move customers across the country from city to city, with long stops for lunches or rests and with restaurants and cafés on the ground, often in railway stations, used to supply food. With the improvement of aircraft technology and the lengthening of flight times, however, came the imperative that multiple meals be served aboard a single non-stop trip, and this is why Pan Am is so significant in the story of in-flight dining; naturally, routes over the sea such as its San Francisco–Honolulu flight, at the time the world's longest flight, did not allow for hop-on/hop-off dining.

While the identity of the first airline to serve hot meals is disputed, Pan Am was certainly the first commercial airline to heat food in-flight, in 1934 on a Sikorsky S-42 flying boat.[12] From 1931 the company's large flying boats comprised its nautically titled Clipper fleet. With increased size came increased passenger numbers. The space, in turn, enabled an on-board pantry with a refrigerator and stove, leading to the development of a galley with a steam table to enable hot meals.[13] In 1936 the company oversaw the first installation of a galley aboard any aircraft: the M130 flying boat. The company's commissary department, which

[11] Ann Whyte, 'The early pursers: Chief cooks, bottlewashers, and in-flight typists', *Clipper* (April 1986).
[12] See, e.g., Oliver Smith, 'Airline food through the ages', http://www.telegraph.co.uk/travel/comment/Airline-food-through-the-ages/ (accessed 11 October 2013) which attributes this first to United Airlines. Lufthansa also claims this first. For Pan Am's claim, see 'History of Pan American World Airways, 1927 to 1956', University of Miami special collections, Pan Am collection no. 341, series I, box 62, folder 2. See also Banks, *Gourmet and Glamor*, 34.
[13] Stirn Groh and Snider Sprecher, 'Dining Aloft', 121–4.

was established several months before the first passengers boarded the M130 and was responsible for the supply of equipment and foodstuffs, worked with company engineers to devise the model of a hot food cabinet, something deemed impractical on aircraft before this point in time.[14] Dinner and breakfast were served in the aircraft's lounge, which was unusually spacious for the time and in which passengers were free to move around, although smoking was not allowed due to the proximity of the fuel tanks. The safety concerns around the risk of conflagration would be thrown into sharp relief by the Hindenburg disaster of 6 May 1937, which marked the end of the airship era and furthered the ascent of the airplane, as discussed later.

As Pan Am grew, it pioneered transoceanic services over the Pacific and Atlantic, further expanding American influence and projecting an expanding American cultural confidence and prestige. Integral to this was the design of the space on the plane where food and drink were served: the lounge. Carl B. Allen – a pioneering pilot, aviation editor at the *New York Herald Tribune* and all-round authority on the industry – wrote admiringly that the lounges on Pan Am's Clippers had 'all the added appointments of a luxurious yacht':

> The ship boasts a ladies' lounge forward and a smoking room aft; its numerous compartments are fitted with comfortable, richly upholstered chairs; the walls are adorned with ingeniously fashioned wood-inlay pictures depicting the history of transportation from the ox cart to the airplane; each window has a roller shade, and there is an individual reading lamp beside every seat.[15]

As this quote illustrates, in the 1930s the airplane was the pinnacle of modernity and the space where food was consumed – the lounge – reflected this. The interior styling described by Carl B. Allen was the work of the renowned American industrial and theatrical designer Norman Bel Geddes who, at the time, occupied the progressive vanguard of the design movement. His 'Futurama' exhibit at the 1939 New York World's Fair – which simulated the experience of flight through elevating spectators on a conveyor belt upwards to an 'airplane eye' vantage point[16] – would gain him great popular acclaim. Geddes was part of the Art Deco design movement and a contemporary, Walter Gropius, the German founder of the Bauhaus movement, would go on to provide the

---

[14] 'History of Pan American World Airways' (1946), University of Miami special collections, Pan Am collection no. 341, series I, box 196, folder 10.
[15] Carl B. Allen, Latin American notes, Carl B. Allen papers, box 3, folder 1, West Virginia and Regional Archives Center (WVRAC), West Virginia University Libraries.
[16] See Adnan Morshed, 'The aesthetics of ascension in Norman Bel Geddes's Futurama', *Journal of the Society of Architectural Historians* 63, 1 (2004), 74–99.

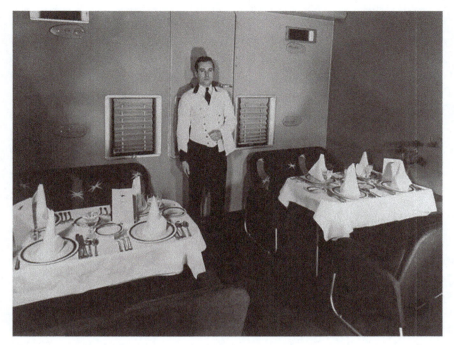

Figure 1.1 The main dining room of the B-314 Clipper (1939). Note the 'Stars and Stripes' upholstery and the purser-as-butler. Courtesy: Foynes Flying Boat and Maritime Museum.

modern, geometric aesthetic of Pan Am's headquarters in New York City (now the MetLife building). As discussed in the following chapter, the interior of Pan Am's cutting-edge M130 (1936) and the main dining room of the B-314 Clipper (1939) were designed by Bel Geddes. The latter featured a 'gay color scheme with a spirited blue pattern on furniture upholstery, rich terracotta carpeting and walls of silvery beige'; the seats, coloured 'Pan Am blue', replicated the stars and stripes of the US flag.[17] When passengers consumed food, then, they did so in an environment symbolizing the globalization of a confident, modernist American culture, one unrestricted by earthbound limitations (Figure 1.1).

Bel Geddes was the natural choice for the dining room's design: prior to working with Pan Am he had come up with designs for 'Air Liner Number 4', a never-realized gargantuan airplane featuring multiple dining rooms, cocktail lounges, a veranda café and a 278-foot-high aerial café which offered

---

[17] Pan American Airways System, 1940, cited in Tony Presland, 'The system of the flying clippers: Designing Pan American Airways' (unpublished MA dissertation, University of Oxford, 2018), 26.

an 'aeroplane view'.[18] The dimensions of 'Air Liner Number 4' hint at not only the bold ambitions of the early airline industry but also the hangover from the luxury ocean liners. Geddes was essentially envisaging a flying *Titanic*. However, in the early days of flight, service on board the flying boats was hindered by the persistent problem of weight constraints. Due to its weight, for example, the amount of ice permitted was severely limited.[19] Fine china and silverware were used in service but owing to the same weight restrictions there was only one set aboard, which had to be washed and dried by the purser after each and every service. The galley of the B-314 was small, meaning that dining operated on a shift system as there was insufficient space in both the dining cabin and galley to serve all the passengers.[20] With galleys featuring ovens and refrigerators, stewards could now prepare meals in-flight, but not everyone was impressed. In terms of passenger comfort aboard the planes of the 1930s, cabin heating was provided but it was 'rather marginal', as one former employee recalled, and there was no air conditioning.[21] This problem was consistent with those of the airships, where attempts to recreate fine dining as experienced on terra firma were hampered by the very cold temperatures inside the helium-powered craft. Betty Trippe, a passenger on the first transatlantic airplane flight to Lisbon in 1939, complained in her diary that 'meals are a real problem as everything is only partially cooked before being put on board and then reheated on a steam table in the tiny galley'. Although anxious to toe the company line, stating that the food was 'delicious and beautifully served', she nonetheless went on to complain that 'due to the altitude, at breakfast eggs and coffee take twelve minutes to boil. Bread gets hard and stale, cream turns sour and because of the problem of weight, only a limited supply of ice can be carried'.[22]

Betty Trippe's in-flight dinner proved more comfortable, though, than the dinner to commemorate Pan Am's historic achievement in conveying passengers across the Atlantic later that same year. At a special banquet held in London, Betty recorded in her diary, the US Ambassador Joseph Kennedy was so disparaging about British Imperial Airways' unsuccessful attempt to complete the first transatlantic passenger crossing that several local dignitaries left their seats around the dinner table in protest. Ambassador Kennedy's

[18]   Morshed, 'The aesthetics of ascension', 83–6.
[19]   Email correspondence with Ken Lownds (Pan Am, 1970–4), 13 January 2018.
[20]   Presland, 'The system of the flying clippers', 33.
[21]   John Borger, 'Transpacific flight: The technical tasks', University of Miami special collections, Pan Am collection no. 341, series I, box 313, folder 6.
[22]   Trippe, *The Diary and Letters*, 113.

arrogance spoke to the fact that it was the United States, and not the old European powers, leading the way in the industry. Britain's Imperial Airways may have advertised seven-course dinners and five-course lunches on its London–Paris route in the mid-1930s, but the United States was outstripping Europe in terms of airplane technology.[23] While Pan Am at this stage only flew Clipper seaplanes, the arrival of the Douglas Corporation's DC-3 in 1936 signalled a move towards greater comfort and safety in flight and a further confirmation that the technological capabilities of the New World were outstripping those of the Old. Previously, as mentioned, the modest comfort and service of air travel was punctuated with stopovers, affording customers the opportunity to eat on the ground in hotels but breaking journeys up into a series of short trips. As many studies indicate, the enjoyment of food is determined by environment and the aerodynamic DC-3 delivered a smoother, soundproofed, climate-controlled experience. Top industrial designers were recruited to outfit the interiors and lounges and rivals of Pan Am's such as American Airlines soon embraced art deco modernism too, right down to the silver-plate flatware cutlery. With the DC-3, Pan Am's domestic competitors were starting to up their game.

Warm meals had, by this stage, become established features of record-breaking long-haul flights such as Pan Am's non-stop San Francisco to Honolulu service, during which passengers were in the air for an entire day for the first time ever.[24] As the Clipper evolved in the early 1940s into an American cultural icon, the staple consumer comforts of American home and kitchen came to be associated with it. The Heinz Corporation ran several adverts featuring meal service in the Clipper, which appeared in *Life* magazine and other publications and in which the 'aristocrat' tomatoes used in its tomato ketchup were said to give a 'delightful lift' to any dish, whether served in the air or on the ground.[25] Linking the Clipper service with a successful brand like Heinz and its recognizable '57 varieties' slogan reinforced a new idea: that air travel could resemble benign domesticity. As noted previously, as a distinctively American brand Pan Am is often remarked to have come second only to Coca Cola, and in these years the soft drink also came to be closely associated with the airline. Other American food brands lined up to associate themselves with the cultural clout of the

---

[23] Paul Jarvis, *British Airways: An Illustrated History* (London: Amberley, 2014), 38.
[24] Tiemeyer, *Plane Queer*, 24.
[25] Larry Weirather, *The China Clipper, Pan American Airways and Popular Culture* (Jefferson, NC: McFarland, 2006), 186.

Clipper, too, most notably Kellogg's, which claimed Pan Am's pilots kept going by eating 'a big bowl of Kellogg's corn flakes' each morning.[26]

The Second World War and the first airborne presidential meal

With the coming of America's involvement in the Second World War (1941–5) Pan Am operated as an instrument of US strategic interests, a 'direct line of communication' for the 'arsenal of democracy', as President Franklin D. Roosevelt put it, with its fleet transporting men and matériel across the world.[27] The expansion of the company's Atlantic and Pacific routes in the war years was vital to America's quiet growth while a neutral power and the successful pursuit of war following the Japanese attack on Pearl Harbor in December 1941. For this service, Trippe symbolically billed the government just one dollar.[28] With the carrying of war cargoes ensuring that the conservation of space became a priority, the company's commissary team toyed with the idea of replacing the hot meal service with box lunches, reverting to the cold food and sandwiches served in the early days of aviation. However, the company's experts ultimately deemed that the saving in space achieved by reverting back to the flying picnic would be negligible and – most importantly – that eating a hot meal made a big psychological difference in terms of 'vitality' and 'morale' for both crew and passenger alike.[29]

While hot meals were retained, the luxury of Pan Am's aircraft cabins now gave way to wartime necessity and priority cargo, including food supplies, was packed into every inch of space. As a worldwide transport system, Pan Am's fleet and its 25,000 employees represented a vital component of the US war effort and shortly after the Japanese attack on Pearl Harbor Clipper routes were transformed into war routes as the company undertook the construction of dozens of new airports across the world. In particular, the company's eleven enormous transoceanic Clippers were vital. This wartime transport of food cargoes proved significant to the Allied war effort and the supplies transported often prevented starvation. Such was the case with the vast quantities of food

---

[26] Van Vleck, *Empire of the Air*, 102.
[27] Cited in Marylin Bender and Selig Altschul, *The Chosen Instrument: Pan Am, Juan Trippe, and the Rise and Fall of an American Entrepreneur* (New York: Simon and Schuster, 1982), 352.
[28] Eugene Dunning, *Voices of My Peers: Clipper Memories* (Nevada City: Clipper Press, 1993), i.
[29] *New Horizons*, February 1943, University of Miami special collections, Pan Am collection no. 341, series I, box 291, folder 10.

and vermin exterminators flown to the Chinese theatre of war in 1943 when plague and famine threatened.[30] Similarly, the wartime experience of Pan Am in flying 650,000 tons of food and fuel from India into China to supply the forces of Chiang Kai-Shek would provide the blueprint for the Berlin airlift of 1948.[31] At Pan Am's various bases employees also contributed to the war effort by starting 'victory gardens', providing a continuous crop of vegetables for Clipper menus.[32] Domestically, greater vegetable production and the consumption of 'substitute foods' was encouraged by all governments during the war due to the decline in supplies of meat and fats: a consequence of both wartime disruption to production and the prioritizing of these foodstuffs for the armed forces. These trends impacted the dinner table. In the United States and other Allied nations, the substitution of peanuts for meats in popular dishes was strongly encouraged and Pan Am's Latin American routes assumed a big role in transporting huge quantities of peanut north to the United States and around the world.[33]

The company's centrality to US military interests meant that some of its employees found themselves casualties of wartime starvation tactics. One such was the company's regional managing director (Far East), Rush Clark, who was based in Manila, Philippines. The nucleus of skilled personnel and planes which Pan Am had based in the region meant that Clark and other Pan Am employees were in a strategically important position and, as battle raged in the Pacific between the United States and Japan, they were not evacuated as civilians but were ordered to remain by the US military: a good example of the blurring of Pan Am's commercial and strategic roles as the US government's 'chosen instrument'. On New Year's Day 1942, with Japanese forces advancing on Manila in a pincer movement, the US military ordered Clark to destroy the Pan Am base so that it did not fall into enemy hands. After torching it, Clark was arrested and interned in a Japanese camp. Food rations for interned Pan Am staff were basic – cracked wheat, fruit and rice – and got progressively worse. Ten months later Clark was surviving on two meals of rice and greens daily and he and colleagues faced systematic starvation as rations decreased month on month. By February 1945 malnourished internees were consuming one handful of rice per day. The

---

[30] 'History of Pan American World Airways, 1927 to 1956', University of Miami special collections, Pan Am collection no. 341, series I, box 62, folder 2.

[31] Derek Leebaert, *Grand Improvisation: America Confronts the British Superpower, 1945–1957* (New York: Farrar, Straus and Giroux, 2018), 153.

[32] 'New Horizons', vol. XIII, no. 3 (January 1943), University of Miami special collections, Pan Am collection no. 341, series I, box 15, folder 9.

[33] Memo from press division on night flying, October 1943, University of Miami special collections, Pan Am collection no. 341, series I, box 64, folder 6.

company maintained salary payments during the three-year internment and Clark attributed the ability of Pan Am staff to borrow money against future wages, and thus to pay camp guards for extra food, as 'the main reason most of the Pan Am people returned … it was the major difference. People who did not have this ability to supplement their food were in a really bad shape at the end [or died]..[34]

Despite its privations, the war did usher in a menu which would come to define the airline's food service: the President Special. In 1943, President Franklin D. Roosevelt flew Pan Am to Casablanca for a famous summit with British Prime Minister Winston Churchill and Free French leader Charles de Gaulle. Roosevelt – who in fact possessed a patrician disdain for Trippe as something of a brash arriviste – celebrated his 61st birthday on board on the way home, a meal service named in the commander-in-chief's honour.[35] Stewards Albert Tuinman and Edward Garcia served Roosevelt (who had also become the first sitting US president ever to fly) a birthday dinner of caviar, celery, olives, turkey, peas, potatoes and coffee as well as a big birthday cake (smuggled aboard, it is alleged, by Captain John McCrea of the President's detail). Roosevelt, recalled a member of the Clipper crew, 'cut his cake with obvious delight' and all aboard enjoyed a champagne toast thereafter.[36] After the war, in honour of this moment, Pan Am's first-class meal service was rebranded 'The President' and the inaugural version of this service was provided aboard the double-deck Boeing 377 'Stratocruiser' in 1948. The President Special menu was designed with professional chefs and, as discussed later, collaboration with culinary experts would be a feature of the industry in the post-war period.

The Second World War would also prove the window of opportunity for a man named William Maxson. History has forgotten William Maxson, but this unusual character was arguably the father of airline food and, consequently, this book shall regularly mention him, too. Quirky, clever and larger than life, Maxson was born in Minnesota in 1889. An unflattering profile of him in the *New Yorker* magazine in 1945 reported that his girth resembled that of Henry VIII and, curiously, divulged that he was left-handed,[37] the intention being, it seems, to encourage readers to view this unconventional self-made man as a crank. After a fourteen-year naval career, Maxson moved his wife and three children to New

[34] Rush S. Clark, 'Japanese Internment Camp – Philippines 1942–5', University of Miami special collections, Pan Am collection no. 341, series I, box 15, folder 19.
[35] Interview with Becky Sprecher, 24 January 2018.
[36] 'New Horizons', vol. XIII, no. 3 (January 1943), University of Miami special collections, Pan Am collection no. 341, series I, box 15, folder 9.
[37] 'Defrosted Dinners', *The New Yorker*, 4 August 1945.

Jersey and there set himself up as an inventor. The W. L. Maxson Corporation produced a number of gadgets, but the most successful was his idea of freezing meals and then oven-heating them in the air: a method which he successfully introduced for US servicemen crossing the Atlantic by plane during the war. Maxson named it, futuristically, the 'The Sky Plate'. His enthusiasm around freezing food was said to have come from his own voracious appetite, which led to his embrace of the new technology of frozen food because it allowed greater quantities of food to be kept. On one occasion, having grown more vegetables than he could eat in the garden of his New Jersey home, he froze the produce. Heating it a year later, he determined that it tasted just as good and promptly swore off fresh food for life.[38] Maxson's work with the US government during the Second World War, providing oven units for military transports, made him rich and Trippe, always keen to embrace innovation, liked what he saw. From 1945, Pan Am's partnership with the Maxson Corporation saw the company work with the oven manufacturer in the design of aircraft, allowing more galley space for Maxson-designed large twelve-plate ovens, electrically operated coffee urns, an ice cube compartment, liquor storage, a sink, ice box and refrigerators.[39] In 1946, as discussed subsequently, Pan Am achieved a revolutionary first when it became the first airline to serve pre-cooked frozen food, which was heated in Maxson convection ovens. The airline meal, as we know it today, had arrived.

Enabling the masses to dine in the clouds

After the war, Pan Am faced increased competition, retaining its status as the United States' international airline but losing its outright monopoly. With United Airlines obtaining routes to Hawaii, Trans World Airlines (TWA) to Europe and Northwest to Alaska, a strong response was needed. That came when Pan Am placed what was at that time the largest commercial aircraft order in history for a fleet of Boeing 377 Stratocruisers. The Stratocruiser was a double-decker luxury aircraft which offered spacious 'Sleeperette' seating and also offered berths (with breakfast in bed) at an additional cost. The most famous feature of the aircraft was its spiral staircase, which led to the bar and roomy lower deck lounge. The

---

[38] Rebecca Maskel, 'He saved navy fliers from spam', *Air and Space Magazine*, 17 May 2019 (www.airspacemag.com/dailyplanet/he-saved-navy-fliers-from-spam-98327183/) (accessed 20 March 2019).
[39] *New Horizons*, April–June 1946, University of Miami special collections, Pan Am collection no. 341, series I, box 291, folder 4.

PAN AM HISTORICAL FOUNDATION

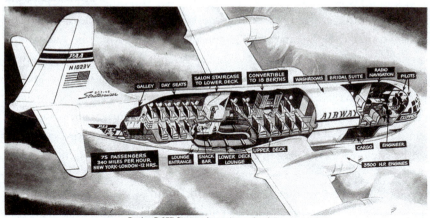

Boeing B-377 Stratocruiser cutaway drawing

Figure 1.2 Inside the Stratocruiser. Courtesy: Pan Am Historical Foundation.

bar and lounge area was mirrored to recreate the ambience of a night club and was full of half circles of snug, well-upholstered seats. On selected long-haul flights, the passenger entryway of the Stratocruiser became a buffet area. Increased space enabled an expanded food service. For first-class passengers, eggs were cooked to order, cracked raw into a tureen, to which milk was added, along with a dash of sherry, before scrambling.[40] The pressurized cabin and higher altitudes of the Stratocruiser were significant aviation innovations, but ones which also affected the consumption of food. The dryness of cabin air, caused by the outside atmosphere, which is compressed and heated before being pumped back into the plane, proved problematic since at higher altitudes the air temperature outside the plane, well below zero, lacked moisture (Figure 1.2). The effect on passengers, it was soon discovered, was marked. With saliva glands working overtime and thirst building, the galley, according to a retired purser 'appeared like an oasis on the desert: the only water hole for miles around'.[41]

The Stratocruiser's pressurized cabin may have dulled taste buds, but food service was still as much about entertainment as taste. Like in a night club, passengers could mosey around, drink in hand, while listening to music. The bar contained a record player which would play ten records selected by senior members of the management team as 'suitable'. Pursers and flight attendants would often subvert the staid record choices by bringing their own records,

[40] Interview with Barbara Sharfstein, 15 January 2018.
[41] Harry Frahm, *Above and Below the Clouds: Recollections* (Frankfurt: Von Goethe, 2013), 79.

but as soon as the plane experienced the slightest turbulence the needle would jump, producing a disagreeably scratchy noise.[42] There were few other forms of entertainment aside from playing cards, drinking and smoking; thus conversation over a long, heavy dinner came to be expected. *Life* magazine breathlessly described the Clippers as 'the best international club in the world' in which – over shrimp cocktail, turtle soup, filet mignon and biscuit tortoni – Archduke Otto, pretender to the defunct Austro-Hungarian throne, dined with Eve Curie, the journalist daughter of the discoverer of radium.[43] Trippe, a Yale man who conducted business in an atmosphere of Scotch-and-cigar clubbiness, would have warmed to this description. But at the same time, although commonly associated with high society, Pan Am's founder had one eye trained on air travel for the masses. Trippe's desire to democratize air travel was a highly significant factor in the direction the airline industry took in the twentieth century, driving his company's post-war success and shaping the development of economy service. Pan Am became the first airline to offer all-expense international air tours in 1932, and its network of hotels – the Intercontinental chain – became a company subsidiary in 1946. By 1947, the time of its twentieth anniversary, Pan Am was a truly international phenomenon, employing nineteen thousand people in sixty-two countries. The following year, after penning a *Reader's Digest* article entitled 'Now You Can Take That Trip Abroad', Trippe introduced economy service, then referred to as 'tourist class'. As with many of Trippe's moves, his inspiration came from the luxury ocean liner industry, which had launched 'tourist class' in the 1920s in reaction to tougher US immigration controls and the emergence of the notion of leisure time as a mass pursuit.

As airlines embraced economy class passengers it was telling that the 1950s ideal of American homeliness permeated aircraft design. The Stratocruiser also featured a 'snack kitchen', which was marketed to resemble home comforts – complimentary sandwiches, bouillon, cookies, fruits, coffee, hot chocolate, fruit juices – a service 'just as at home' where passengers could snack at any time, 'only here you don't have to soft-foot it to the refrigerator', as a company press release quipped.[44] The reference is significant: refrigerators had, at the time, just become a fixture of the American kitchen, accompanying rising affluence, suburbanization and 'scientific housekeeping'.[45] Since it was considered odd to

[42] Frahm, *Above and Below the Clouds*, 48.
[43] Cited in Bender and Altschul, *The Chosen Instrument*, 344.
[44] 'Welcome aboard your Clipper', University of Miami special collections, Pan Am collection no. 341, series I, box 108, folder 14.
[45] Susanne Freidberg, *Fresh: A Perishable History* (Cambridge, MA: Belknap, 2009), 45.

'enter the parlor through the kitchen' the galley was located at the rear of the plane, providing a psychological boost to passengers, who were now served from behind. This stopped them from fidgeting hungrily while watching their food being prepared, recalled a purser.[46] By 1954 flying had become the principal mode of foreign travel for Americans and the founder of Pan Am envisioned legions of ordinary Americans with disposable incomes being able to avail of 'two dollar dinners', served with wine and cognac, as they journeyed to foreign locations like Madrid and Paris.[47]

Such globalizing ambitions coincided with improved flight technology, meaning faster flights and more passengers. With the expansion of the airline industry also came greater price differentials and these were reflected in Pan Am's newly rebranded no-frills offering: Rainbow Service (1953). Although Pan Am came to be associated with luxury, the company's commitment to economy service was reiterated by its founder, with Trippe stating that a 'luxury service to carry the well-to-do at high prices' had inevitably given way to 'the average man at what he can afford to pay'.[48] Initially, though, Rainbow Service featured only cold food. This changed as a result of an intriguing episode which industry insiders referred to as the 'sandwich war' of 1958.

The 'sandwich war' was fought over the new phenomenon of the economy class passenger who, in 1958, was officially recognized by the International Air Transport Association (IATA, the body regulating global commercial aviation) as occupying a separate travel class. As part of the formal distinction of economy class, the IATA had agreed with airlines that they would only serve food to economy class customers that was 'simple, cold and inexpensive': in other words, a sandwich. However, as the battle to recruit more economy class passengers raged, Pan Am noted that three of its main international rivals – KLM, Air France and Swissair – had started to entice the masses by serving hot food in economy and successfully protested to the IATA. After a meeting of the world's airlines at the Washington Hotel, London, the IATA duly restricted economy class food to cold offerings, even going so far as to prohibit overly garnished sandwiches. This latter stipulation, which appears extremely fastidious, reflected the anxiety of the muscular American airlines – Pan Am and TWA – that the European competition was offering better food than them. Scandinavian Airlines (SAS)

---

[46] 'Mile-High Kitchen' (1950), University of Miami special collections, Pan Am collection no. 341, series I, box 108, folder 3.
[47] Bender and Altschul, *The Chosen Instrument*, 470.
[48] 'History of Pan American World Airways, 1927 to 1956', University of Miami special collections, Pan Am collection no. 341, series I, box 62, folder 2.

had ingeniously turned the 'simple, cold and inexpensive' stipulation to their advantage, offering sixteen varieties of smørrebrød: the open-faced, lavishly garnished sandwiches popular in the Nordic countries consisting of rye bread topped with cold cuts, fish or cheese. SAS took out adverts that quite obviously took aim at the inferior sandwiches offered by their big American rivals, boasting 'on our planes you won't find rubbery indigestibles wrapped in cellophane'.[49]

While Pan Am and TWA then succeeded in getting the IATA to issue a considerable fine to SAS, their apparent victory in the 'sandwich war' would prove pyrrhic. The IATA's ruling that smørrebrød could continue to be served as long as two-and-a-half centimetres of the bread remained visible was quite clearly a petty one, and SAS duly revelled in the public relations triumph, taking out adverts claiming that it would rather pay the fine than lower its standards. Insofar as the 'sandwich war' was a conflict between the food cultures of North America and Europe, the latter was the ultimate victor. This was demonstrated three years later when the IATA overturned its original austere ruling, permitting hot food in economy.[50] Pan Am was forced to react. Its food offerings in economy class soon developed to the extent that some proved as appealing as first-class options, stuffed guinea hen being one of the favourites.[51] Given what is now known about how altitude impairs taste buds, especially with blander dishes, it is likely that the rich and succulent nature of dishes like this secured their popularity. For the average person, the cumulative effect of all this was that flying was becoming a lot less unpleasant. Now, in economy class, like first class, food was served on a plate with entrées and accompaniments cooked separately. In an era predating meal carts, flight attendants would carry trays individually by hand, placing the meals – each finished with a signature garnish of parsley – straight to the passenger's lap.[52] For some economy fliers, this was their first experience of anything like restaurant service.

As the 'sandwich war' illustrates, the pan American ideal of air travel as a universalist experience for all was still marked by elitism and division along class lines. Although his Hispanic name often led people to believe otherwise, Trippe's antecedents were exclusively northern European and, like wife Betty, he was a product of the post-Civil War so-called Gilded Age of US affluence. Trippe's wealthy upbringing placed him in a social circle that was firmly white, Anglo-Saxon and Protestant (WASP) and which tended to coalesce along class

[49] '1950s: The great sandwich war', *Scandinavian Traveller*, 25 March 2016.
[50] 'Dining Up', *The New Yorker*, 22 July 1961.
[51] Interview with Barbara Sharfstein, 15 January 2018.
[52] Stirn Groh and Snider Sprecher, 'Dining Aloft', 121–4.

and race lines in order to keep the 'wrong' people out of 'society', imitating older European ways of stratifying the classes, not least through an emphasis on dining etiquette, table manners and French conventions around food.[53] This sort of social stratification was replicated on the great ocean liners to ensure more affluent passengers did not dine alongside the less well off. Hence, Pan Am's position in the 'sandwich war' was that economy passengers would be restricted to cold food whereas those who had paid top dollar for their ticket would be treated to hot meals.

At the same time, Trippe's early championing of economy class in the first place is revealing of the company's all-embracing ethos under his leadership. While elitism was an inherent feature of Pan Am, Trippe's emphasis on 'the average man' simultaneously harked back to an earlier republican ethos around food and transport reminiscent of the great American 'palace hotels' of the mid-nineteenth century: enormous buildings where members of the general public could sleep and eat well for an all-inclusive price. In seeking to create large flying hotels, there was a clear lineage between Bel Geddes's designs for his gargantuan 'Air Liner Number 4' and Trippe's democratic embrace of 'the average man'. In many ways, then, Trippe's Pan Am saw itself as collapsing the distinctions between the Old and the New World, and not least – as we shall see – through dining styles, granting the 'average man' a rare glimpse of culinary 'civilization'. That the company had effectively been forced into this embrace of a more sophisticated and transnational cuisine by the 'sandwich war' and its aftermath would be conveniently forgotten.

Nothing symbolized better the fact that the masses were gradually being granted access to 'the club' like the Boeing 707. From 1958, the 707 jet engine significantly cut journey times and laid the groundwork for the expansion of mass tourism. The advent of the jet age would both limit and expand the potential for good food service.[54] If greater passenger numbers meant that the sense of exclusivity in food service was diminished somewhat, cart service was introduced to enhance the entertainment value on long flights. Moreover, the jet engine cut out the vibration experienced with the piston engine, making in-flight service more manageable. A defiant Pan Am press release of 1960 derided the ' "prophets" who said that jet speed would reduce the desire for in-flight service',

---

[53] See Susan Williams, *Savory Suppers and Fashionable Feasts: Dining in Victorian America* (New York: Pantheon, 1985); David Shields, *The Culinarians: Lives and Careers from the First Age of American Fine Dining* (Chicago: University of Chicago Press, 2017).

[54] Guillaume de Syon, 'Airmeals: We are what we eat, but what happens when we fly?', *Sabor* 1 (2013), digital issue.

pointing out that 'the lack of vibration of jet aircraft' was 'conducive to gracious dining and delectable meals made possible by the jets' modern ovens and other galley equipment'.[55] Staff, however, found the 707 jet airplane disappointingly short on space. Food service was likened to preparing 'numerous TV dinners in your broom closet'; the galley was confined and swelteringly hot, and bruises and burns were common injuries; the pre-cooked frozen meals which William Maxson had pioneered were wrapped in rugged-edged aluminium, resulting in numerous cuts which even the improvisation of wearing rubber gloves could not guard against.[56]

Although several European airlines introduced jet planes before Pan Am, the company's promotional material conveyed American ownership of the technology and the possibilities for transnational exchange that it opened up. Pan Am's marketing around the 707 stressed the revolutionary potential of mass travel by jet aircraft, promising customers that '*yesterday's dream* of dinner in Paris and theatre in New York is a *reality today!*'[57] This was part of a publicity blitz around jets conducted by the company's advertising agency JWT which, at a cost of $1.5 million, eclipsed any previous airline advertising assaults. Availing of the best marketing men America had to offer, the company soon set about broadening its appeal, turning its attention to women and children. While previously flying had been a largely male preserve, the company now appealed to the housewife as well, promising a 'cook-out above the clouds' that would liberate them from their 'slaving over a hot stove routine', and to children, who would receive a miniature plastic 707 if they sent in their Kellogg's corn flakes box top.[58]

The upper lounge

While shorter flight times demanded greater efficiency and standardization of food service, the purser was still important. Prior to take-off, and at the same time as the pilots were undertaking pre-departure checks, the purser would hold a briefing for the cabin crew, informing them of the special dietary requirements of any VIPs on the flight, any unusual meal requests from passengers and

[55] University of Miami special collections, Pan Am collection no. 341, series I, box 62, folder 3.
[56] Frahm, *Above and Below the Clouds*, 48.
[57] Pan Am promotional brochure, '707 Jet Clippers' (1958, courtesy of Becky Sprecher). For design, advertising and shorter journey times see also Matthias Hühne, *Pan Am History, Design and Identity* (Berlin: Callisto, 2017).
[58] Van Vleck, *Empire of the Air*, 259.

ensuring that the provisioning of food and drinks corresponded to passenger and crew statistics. Ultimately, it was still up to the purser to ensure that there were enough glasses, plates, cups and items of silverware on board to ensure good service. Arguably, though, some of the charm of flying was beginning to rub off as it became a mass pursuit. A 1961 article in the *New Yorker* magazine sought to explain why airlines were now devoting so much time to marketing around food, reminding readers that all commercial airplanes shared basic technological features. They were just 'winged cylinders off a standard assembly line', piloted by 'a quick-thinking young man, and aided by a crew of equal merit'. It was exactly this uniformity, the article claimed, that made airline advertising focus on 'such peripheral matters as cuisine'.[59]

In ruthlessly stripping away the marketing spin, the article had hit on something. In was against this commercially undesirable backdrop of 'uniformity', in 1965, that Pan Am's executives decided that public demand and advanced technology called for a new type of aircraft twice as large as the 707. Pan Am's – and thereby the United States' – original advantage over European competition lay in the size and efficiency of its Clipper fleet; if the Americans were to retain the edge over the Europeans, a similarly big and bold new aircraft was needed. The company therefore played a key role in engineering and designing the world's largest commercial air transport – the Boeing 747. At a 1966 business council dinner at the White House with Lyndon B. Johnson (incidentally, the first president in thirty-eight years with whom the well-connected Trippe had been unable to secure a one-to-one meeting), the man who embodied Pan Am pressed the national economic gains that would derive from the manufacture of the new jumbo jet.[60] The company he had founded had just celebrated welcoming its fifty millionth passenger and, mindful of increased passenger numbers, Trippe had set his heart on a double-decker airplane. Johnson, for his part, liked what he heard. However, meetings with Boeing engineers were to convince Trippe that a full double-decker aircraft was unsafe because it would take people too long to descend from the upper deck in an emergency. Eventually, Boeing's engineers convinced Pan Am's supremo of the benefits of what was essentially a single-deck aircraft with greater space than ever before on the main deck. Still, Trippe got his way in insisting that Boeing make the 747 *technically* a double-decker, with a smaller 'upper bulge' capable of holding around forty passengers.[61] The upper

[59] 'Dining Up', *The New Yorker*, 22 July 1961.
[60] Bender and Altschul, *The Chosen Instrument*, 504.
[61] Joe Sutter, *747: Creating the World's First Jumbo Jet and Other Adventures from a Life in Aviation* (New York: Smithsonian, 2006), 102.

bulge would become the aircraft's fabled upper lounge. Many passengers who subsequently enjoyed the exclusive dining experience of the upper lounge would fail to realize that it was safety considerations rather than elitism-by-design that dictated the nature of the space in which they ate (Figure 1.3).

Figure 1.3 Pan Am founder Juan Trippe (1899–1981). Wikimedia Commons.

From 1969 onwards – the year after Trippe stepped down as company president – the Boeing 747 became the standard Pan Am aircraft and the company's inaugural 747 flight from New York to London ushered in the second phase of the jet age. The 747's major selling point was the comfort and convenience its spaciousness allowed. At its introduction, the 747 was the widest and roomiest plane around, allowing greater comfort for passengers and food servers alike. It was equipped with six galleys, capable of providing meal service to up to 362 passengers, as well as wider in-and-out galleys pre-packed with snacks and beverages. Serving time was reduced by 30 per cent as flight attendants used rolling carts instead of carrying meals one at a time.[62] On the 707s there was one cart per service, whereas the 747 had two carts – one for each aisle. Foldable carts containing 36 full meals were a feature, meaning less running back and forth by flight attendants carrying trays, and a quicker food operation than ever before.

If abundance and variety of food distinguished the 747, another notable feature of the new jets was the increased altitude of 45,000 feet: a mile higher than jets had ever flown before. Yet these higher altitudes, of course, meant that taste buds were further inhibited. The low humidity led to the drying out of nasal passages and the air pressure also led to the desensitization of taste. Airlines therefore increasingly opted for stronger-tasting food – with more flavoursome sauces[63] – and this is reflected in the changing composition of menus. A typical Pan Am President Special menu of the 1970s offered as mains sole meunière (in a rich brown butter sauce with parsley and lemon), hen marinated in madeira sauce and steak drenched in butter. Indian madras sauce also increasingly made its way into menus from this period.[64] In the 1970s the company developed its 'Fear of Flying Program' for nervous flyers, a central part of which was the provision of 'comfort' foods in-flight: sweet rolls and coffee and other 'treats'.[65] The unusual blending of haute cuisine with comfort foods was becoming a feature of airline food and the mixing of mains and desserts from different cultures, resulting in hybrid menus and expanded choice, was another distinctively transnational feature of feeding in the air.

[62] Lynn Homan and Thomas Reilly, *Images of Aviation: Pan Am* (Stroud: Arcadia, 2000), 111.
[63] Guillaume de Syon, 'Is it really better to travel than to arrive? Airline food as a reflection of consumer anxiety', in Lawrence C. Rubin (ed.), *Food for Thought: Essays on Eating and Culture* (Jefferson, NC: McFarland, 2008), 277–93.
[64] President special menu 1970s, University of Miami special collections, Pan Am collection no. 341, series I, box 497, folder 10.
[65] See University of Miami special collections, Pan Am collection no. 341, series I, box 193, folder 29.

These developments were underpinned by the market conditions of the airline industry in the 1970s, which drove established carriers like Pan Am to concentrate ever more on the quality and diversity of their food offerings. The British and French governments liberalized their aviation markets in the early years of the decade, leading to a proliferation of new carriers offering high capacity, low prices and low service. The pay-off for the notoriously poor food on these budget airlines (which, in contrast to food on the grand older airlines, had to be paid for) was the cheap price of transatlantic travel. This led, in turn, to the development of a special economy class – business class – between first class at the front and economy at the rear. While international competitors like the Australian carrier Qantas used the term 'business class', British Airways referred to it as 'Club Class', and in 1978 Pan Am branded it 'Clipper Class'. The heritage reference was telling. Even the likes of the upstart British discount carrier Laker Airways had evolved from no-frills beginnings to offer a 'Regency Service' of leather seats, Wedgwood china, champagne and free meals.[66] The older and more expensive airlines responded by accentuating the established high quality of their food.

Therefore, the careful and ornate presentation of food was another way in which Pan Am sought to differentiate itself from its rivals and the company aimed to not only imitate but also surpass the opulence of European and Japanese carriers. With international competition for top-tier customers increasingly reliant on the allure of exclusivity, much time was dedicated to menu design and presentation and many of the 747 menus were works of art, featuring designs by renowned designers such as the Chinese-American artist Dong Kingman. The food in first class was presented on china and glassware produced by dinnerware companies such as the American-Japanese Noritake, the American-German Rosenthal or the German Bauscher Weiden.[67] Such was the consistent quality of Pan Am's ware that one account recalls how on 8 December 1941, one day after the bombing of Pearl Harbor, the Pan Am flying boat base at Wake Island was attacked; Pan Am employees, with scant regard for their personal safety, reputedly rushed into the burning hotel building to save the precious dishes from destruction. The quality of ware continued into the later years, with gold-plated knives, forks and spoons a feature of food service aboard the 747. Right up until the company's closure, Pan Am still prepared main meals on board; a favourite among cabin crew was chateaubriand (roast tenderloin of

---

[66] Foss, *Food in the Air and Space*, 36.
[67] Lou Berman, 'Pan Am's Haute Cuisine: Praised to the High Heavens', *Clipper* (March 2012), 7.

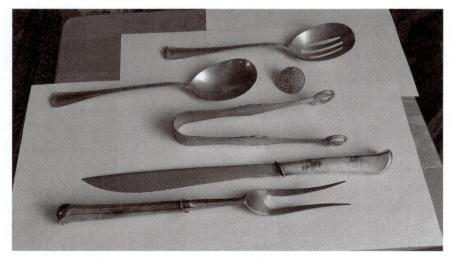

Figure 1.4 Serving implements of the 747. Courtesy: Winnie Omodt.

beef)[68] and caviar, an ever-present in first class. Galleys felt like proper kitchens with on-board utensils including a full carving set, meat thermometer, pepper grinder, ice cream spoon, tongs, mittens, and serving spoons and forks – serving implements since removed from most commercial flights after the 9/11 attacks of 2001 (Figure 1.4).[69]

The end of the Golden Age

And yet, in many ways, Juan Trippe's retirement in 1969, coinciding with the birth of the second 'jet age', had already signalled the end of aviation's 'golden age' as immortalized by Frank Sinatra's 'Come Fly with Me'. Paradoxically, the death of the golden age was symbolized by a christening: that of the company's first 747 in 1970 by First Lady Pat Nixon. Instead of breaking the traditional champagne bottle over the aircraft, the ceremony involved Mrs Nixon pulling a handle which triggered a photogenic spray of fake champagne from an unseen source onto the plane's nose.[70] Airline service was losing some of its decadent, if patrician, charm. In the 1970s the industry was to open up, becoming more widely available to the general public and dampening the air of exclusivity that

---

[68] Email correspondence with Debbi Fuller, 11 January 2018.
[69] Stirn Groh and Snider Sprecher, 'Dining Aloft', 121–4.
[70] James Kaplan, *The Airport* (New York: Morrow, 1994), 76.

had always surrounded it. In the 1950s the United States' seven domestic carriers had convinced Congress to restrict Pan Am to international (non-domestic) flights, a ruling which infuriated Trippe. Although the decision served to enhance his company's exclusively international image, unlike in the early days Pan Am was no longer the United States' sole international carrier, even if it remained the largest and most influential.

In an increasingly competitive marketplace and with the increased capacity of the 747, food service became even more demanding. With computerized scheduling, crew layover times were also cut – from three or four days to the shortest possible breaks calculated from the minimum eight hours' rest time. A former flight attendant who served on the inaugural 747 flight in 1970, on an aircraft packed full of dignitaries and journalists in convivial mood, recalled the 'hellish' experience of preparing five different cuts of meat all cooked to the different specifications of hundreds of people imbued with drunken entitlement.[71] While a grandiose project, the 747 was also emblematic of the demise of air travel in the 1970s: the jumbo jet burdened airlines with debt in a time of global financial contraction and created the now familiar 'herd' experience for travellers in coach, emphasizing an imperative of quantity and mass production over quality. Speaking back in 1941, Trippe had cautioned against overlooking the role of the flight steward: 'with sometimes as many as thirty-two passengers to care for, in addition to the crew, he is by no means the least busy member of the ship's complement'.[72] Thirty years later, with four hundred bodies now occupying just one plane, the flight attendant was busier than ever.

From the 1970s onwards, with increased competition, achieving economies became a greater priority for airlines. In 1980, though, Pan Am splurged on the acquisition of Miami-based National Airlines; the move proved controversial as well as costly and the corporate cultures all but incompatible. Then, in the middle of the decade, Pan Am shocked many in the United States by turning down long-term American partner Boeing in favour of a large order of planes from the European consortium Airbus. Although the 747 remained in service on long-haul transoceanic routes, it was felt that the aircraft was too large to operate on flights to and from destinations in Latin America, as economic conditions and passenger numbers fell in that market.[73] This reversion to the smaller Airbus

---

[71] Interview with Margie Thompson, 15 March 2018.
[72] Juan Trippe, 'Ocean air transport', 29th Wilbur Wright Memorial Lecture, 17 June 1941. Truman Library, George C. Neal papers, Pan American Airways file, box 26–8.
[73] Transcript of Airbus press conference, 20 September 1984, Pan Am collection no. 341, series I, box 93, folder 2.

aircraft underlined how the company's drive for economy in an increasingly competitive marketplace had nudged the spacious and comfortable 747 aside. While the 747 went on to remain a desirable product for other airlines, Pan Am's over-investment in it ultimately proved uneconomic. This move, for many, marked the definite end of Pan Am's 'golden age' of airline dining and, with it, any pretensions to recreate the grand dining luxury of the ocean liners. As if to underline the fact, a regular fault developed with the toilet vacuum pump on the Airbus A310 which, after heavy use following food service, would become stuck and begin flushing continuous and very noisily.[74] Small but telling economy measures began to creep into food service. The Christmas dinner offered on all flights airborne on 25 December was maintained, but in 1986 the special greeting cards accompanying it were axed, along with the complimentary seasonal eggnog.[75] Complaints about cost-cutting's negative impact on the quality of food also increased; in a karmic reminder of the 'sandwich war', one common gripe was that there was insufficient amount of turkey on croissant sandwiches.[76] As the sell-off of assets gathered pace, management demanded that employees work longer hours for less pay, which in turn negatively impacted standards of service. Staff were soon urged to salvage all non-perishable items such as packets of sugar, cream, plastic cups and swizzle sticks in order that they be re-used on subsequent flights.[77]

These economies were telling of the fact that whereas in the past Pan Am's operating budgets for catering and other forms of research and development far outpaced its rivals, these were now being slashed. Pan Am's mythic air of exceptionalism was giving way to the reality of a standardized and globally competitive airline industry in which the company was no longer the dominating colossus it once was. It would not be long before what was arguably the greatest airline the world has ever known was no more. The bombing of Pan Am Clipper *Maid of the Seas* over the Scottish town of Lockerbie on 21 December 1988 would prove decisive. One historian describes the impact of the atrocity through a metaphor which, although mixed, captures its disastrous effect: 'if advertising and public relations are the air in the soufflé of an airline's image – and the necessary underpinning for the kabuki of commercial air travel – commercial

[74] Pan Am Monthly operational bulletin, vol. 18, no. 6, July 1988, University of Miami digital collections, Pan Am material.

[75] Pan Am Monthly operational bulletin, vol. 16, no. 13, December 1986, University of Miami digital collections, Pan Am material.

[76] Pan Am Monthly operational bulletin, vol. 17, no. 12, December 1987, University of Miami Libraries digital collections, Pan Am material.

[77] Susan Timper, 'Catering to customer expectations', *Clipper* (November 1990), 4.

airline crashes are the very worst public relations conceivable'.[78] But the death of Pan Am had been coming for a longer time, with one former employee recalling that throughout the 1980s 'Pan Am was gettin' shabbier and shabbier … they'd run out of juice and food – I know they ran out of food for employees a lot of times.'[79] Due to wear, it was even proving impossible to properly clean food stains and crumbs from the iconic sheepskin seat covers in 747 first class. More and more passengers were complaining of discoloration due to long-accumulated food debris.[80] The cracks were starting to show. Following the failure of a hoped-for merger with Delta Airlines, Pan Am suffered an inglorious end, declaring bankruptcy in January 1991. A more fitting food-based metaphor for the airline's demise reflects the fact that the company had over-reached itself in an intensely competitive era. Pan Am, in the end, died suffering from obesity.

[78] James Kaplan, *The Airport* (New York: Morrow, 1994), 76.
[79] Les Radley, quoted in Kaplan, *The Airport*, 102.
[80] Pan Am Monthly operational bulletin, vol. 17, no. 7, July 1987, University of Miami Libraries digital collections, Pan Am material.

2

'Revolutionary Advancement': The science behind food by air

Recollections of the food of the 'golden age' of flying are often rose-tinted, based around the abundance of food and drink. This promise of abundant consumption was a distinctly American theme, bound up with the cultural, economic and political leadership role assumed internationally by the United States after the Second World War. Indeed, many standard features of the airline industry today – from the science of airborne food safety, to the materials and utensils used, to food heating, refrigeration, preservation and packaging processes – can be traced back to post-war American-led scientific achievements. In short, the carefree elegance of the Pan Am dining experience was underpinned by hard science. More than that, the scientific innovations enabling the possibility of in-flight dining would have global implications. The unique technological innovations of the airline industry (outlined briefly in the previous chapter) would impact food science more broadly and, as discussed in this chapter in greater depth, place the United States at the forefront of scientific modernity.

Hydroponics

Interestingly, one of the most important of Pan Am's global food legacies took place not in the air but on the ground, where the company made an important contribution towards the development of a science that would help address the problem of adequate international food supply: hydroponics. In the 1930s Juan Trippe was keen to establish an air service between the United States and China, but the US–China journey was so lengthy that it required a mid-Pacific layover for refuelling and maintenance. Following research, Trippe decided that the atolls of Midway and Wake would be ideal for this purpose and wrote to the US Navy requesting a lease. Wake, a tiny and isolated territory 1,200 miles from the much larger Midway, was formally claimed by the United States in 1899 but in Trippe's day it lay deserted and largely forgotten. After consideration, and largely thanks to the backdrop of Japanese expansion in the Pacific, in March 1935 the US government granted Pan Am permission to start building on both islands. As mentioned previously, Pan Am would prove a vital tool in America's coming Pacific conflict with Japan. The worsening geopolitical situation ensured that Trippe, the consummate expansionist, once again won out against the isolationists on Capitol Hill.

A charted freighter, SS *North Haven*, duly embarked for Wake and Midway as a Pan Am vessel, laden with a four-month supply of food and 120 laborers and engineers, many of whom were elite university graduates keen for adventure. Once they had arrived, however, maintaining food supply proved problematic. Food came from chartered ships which arrived infrequently and had insufficient refrigeration facilities. It was here that Pan Am's newly formed commissary department led the way in scientific innovation around food preservation, providing dried ice to the ships in order to supplement the refrigeration process.[1] The greater goal, meanwhile, was to develop agriculture on the atolls themselves. Trippe's teams consequently pioneered hydroponic gardening (growing crops in an aquatic environment) on Wake and Midway. This method was necessary because the soil was so poor that vegetables fit for human consumption did not grow naturally.[2] The process was aided by the *North Haven*, which brought a large tonnage of rich topsoil to the atolls.

As the company's official records put it,

> Not the residents of the dust bowl alone know the hardships of soil erosion and plant destruction by the sun's heat. The colonizers in the cause of aviation on Midway have been wrestling with the same problem. [But] onto the desk of a department head at the Pan American Airways Alameda terminal one day last week there was dropped evidence by air mail that the midpacific area has solved its agrarian problem … a sample of a six-day old tame oat measuring five inches … with roots fully four inches long. This without any watering![3]

---

[1] 'History of Pan American World Airways' (1946), University of Miami special collections, Pan Am collection no. 341, series I, box 196, folder 10.

[2] For Pan Am's concept of the 'sea-as-runway' and negotiating landing rights with foreign governments see N. D. B. Connolly, 'Timely innovations: Planes, trains and the "whites only" economy of a Pan-American city', *Urban History* 36, 2 (2009), 243–61.

[3] 'China: Background', University of Miami special collections, Pan Am collection no. 341, series I, box 61, folder 7.

That nine-inch oat would justify the company's embrace of hydroponics. Around the same time, young US scientists from the Rockefeller Foundation were carrying out similar experiments in Mexico, developing the high-yielding and disease-resistant varieties of wheat which signalled the start of the so-called 'Green Revolution'. The resultant increase in agricultural production, and concomitant reduction in famine, would completely transform the global food system.[4] Growing crops in such an inhospitable environment was remarkable not only as an episode in the history of food science, then, it also played an important role in bolstering the idea that Pan Am's raison d'être was not merely profit but also civilizational improvement. It was a good example of the dovetailing of imperial and universal goals in the 'American Century'. On the one hand, the development and occupation of Wake and Midway aided US expansionism in an era of competitive nationalism; on the other, it addressed the common human desire to attain productivity from barren land in order to prevent the widening of the gap between the world's food supply and the demands of its growing population. It was justified in such terms by Trippe himself who, addressing the Royal Aeronautical Society in London in 1941, spoke of Wake as a 'tiny low-lying V-shaped atoll, a thousand miles from the nearest land ... there was no vegetation save matted underbrush, no fresh water, no food, no shelter'; its unlikely cultivation, said Trippe, proved that aviation could be 'a constructive force in world civilization'.[5]

Trippe was speaking during the Second World War, a time in which the airplane was more associated with destruction than civilizational progress. Commercial transit to Midway and Wake was interrupted by the war, but the first civilian passengers to make the stopover did so on Pan Am's San Francisco to Manila route. On the atolls, the passengers were encouraged to go angling for their dinner, one of the members of the inaugural press flight bringing in a parrot fish weighing 112 pounds. Journalists wondered at the thriving vegetable garden, cows, pigs and chickens on land previously only inhabited by seabirds and rats. After departure, 191 miles out from Midway, the crossing of the international date line was marked by a beefsteak dinner aboard the plane. The beefsteak celebration may have mirrored older nautical dining traditions – traditionally, such a dinner commemorated a ship's

---

[4] See Leon Hesser, *The Man Who Fed the World: Nobel Peace Prize Laureate Norman Borlaug and His Battle to End World Hunger* (New York: Park East Press, 2010).
[5] Juan Trippe, 'Ocean air transport', 29th Wilbur Wright Memorial Lecture, 17 June 1941. Truman Library, George C. Neal papers, Pan American Airways file, box 26–8.

crossing of the equator – but the whole experience had a novel, cutting-edge quality to it.[6]

In the midst of wartime starvation, Pan Am's activity on the atolls seemed to strike a rare tone of humanitarian progress. Cultivating food on the atolls was not without its problems, though. As usual, the fanfare surrounding the progressive benefits of the imperial mission would drown out the difficulties and disappointments. Pan Am's operations manager at Wake reported in late 1940 that 'the chicken ranch is a flop' and that the importance of hydroponics had been over-hyped, admitting 'we've publicized the thing so much that we can't really back out even if we wanted to'.[7] Another problem was the availability of drinking water. Water shortages on Wake saw company employees resort to making stills, but the limited supplies had to be rationed among employees and they became reliant upon collecting rainwater.[8] Nonetheless, Pan Am employees on Wake were provisioned with the latest in kitchen technology – electric refrigerators and electric dishwashers – the latter considered 'a very sanitary precaution' by the company medical team because 'it automatically assures pretty good sterilization of utensils'.[9] And despite the teething problems, the recent backdrop of the 'Dirty Thirties' – when the Dust bowl droughts wrought great ecological and agricultural damage to the North American prairies – provided justification to Pan Am's progress in exploring alternative forms of cultivation.

Modernism versus Traditionalism

Pioneering science was taking place in the air, too. As detailed above, food was warmed in the air for the first time in the mid-1930s aboard the Sikorsky S-42, with a glycol circulating system connected from the galley to one of the engines providing heat to a steam table unit.[10] Shortly thereafter, in 1936, the company's commissary and engineering departments collaborated on installing the first airline cooking galleys aboard M130 aircraft. Continued research resulted in the utilization of exhaust heat and the evolution of the airplane steam table, which

---

[6] Staff Correspondent, 'Typhoon holds China clipper an extra day at Wake Island', *New York Herald Tribune*, 12 October 1936. Carl B. Allen papers, box 8, folder 3, WVRAC.

[7] John Leslie to Clarence Young, 7 November 1940, University of Miami special collections, Pan Am collection no. 341, series I, box 13, folder 2.

[8] Interview with George Kuhn, July 1958, University of Miami special collections, Pan Am collection no. 341, series I, box 15, folder 13.

[9] John Leslie to Clarence Young, 7 November 1940, University of Miami special collections, Pan Am collection no. 341, series I, box 13, folder 2.

[10] Whyte, 'The early pursers: Chief cooks, bottlewashers, and in-flight typists'.

was used to heat food. The steam table's heat was supplied by ethylene glycol fluid heated in engine exhaust stacks and piped to the galley, from where the steward served hot meals.[11] Later aircraft built on this early innovation. The Boeing 314, which was introduced in 1939, came equipped with an icebox and ample cooking and preparation space, as well as a variety of innovative methods for heating food, such as steam tables, pressure cookers and electric fan-assisted ovens.[12] A central consideration around food service remained general passenger comfort, particularly ensuring that it was not too cold on board. This was enhanced in 1939 with the introduction of air conditioning – referred to clumsily in the literature of the time as a 'supercharging, heating and ventilating system'.[13] This early research into customer service led the company's commissary department to conclude that serving hot meals was desirable but that certain dietetic principles needed to be followed when serving hot food in the air (Figure 2.1). As a result of these studies Pan Am's commissary superintendent published an authoritative volume on food safety entitled 'Flight Food'.[14]

Similarly, Pan Am's collaboration with the leading figures of the Art Deco movement went beyond aesthetics. Industrial designer Norman Bel Geddes's involvement with the M130 (1936) and B-314 (1939) also led to scientific innovation around food service. It is easy to see the modernist scientific appeal of Art Deco, which took its name from the 1925 international exhibition of modern and decorative arts in Paris, to America's leading international air carrier. Bel Geddes had a hand in the M130's dinnerware, designing plates and saucers with a vacuum bottom which allowed them to cling to the table, overcoming some of the problems associated with crockery smashing due to turbulence. Bel Geddes sought to improve on his designs with the B-314 and, once again, food preparation and consumption was given scientific attention. This time, he included overhead lighting in the galley for greater visibility and instructed that the counters be covered with vinylite plastic, which helped with cleaning. Reflecting Art Deco's penchant for plastics, linoleum replaced carpet in the galley too, which made it easier to clean up spills.[15] Achieving cleanliness was more than a sanitary goal; it symbolized the thrusting, modernist cultural

[11] 'History of Pan American World Airways' (1946), University of Miami special collections, Pan Am collection no. 341, series I, box 196, folder 10.

[12] Foss, *Food in the Air and Space*, 38.

[13] Harold Mansfield memo, 20 March 1940, University of Miami special collections, Pan Am collection no. 341, series I, box 106, folder 5.

[14] 'History of Pan American World Airways' (1946), University of Miami special collections, Pan Am collection no. 341, series I, box 196, folder 10.

[15] James Trautman, *Pan American Clipper: The Golden Age of Flying Boats* (Erin, Ontario: Boston Mills, 2007), 54.

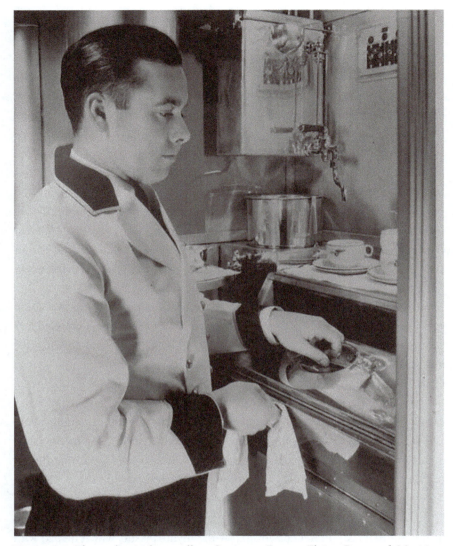

Figure 2.1 The early airplane galley. Courtesy: Foynes Flying Boat and Maritime Museum.

psyche of the time, in which the dirty surfaces of pre-design-era products signified corruption, impotence and an unsanitary germ-rich environment.[16]

The blending of the local and the global, the artisan and the mass produced, would recur later in Pan Am's transnational food service. Within the company,

---

[16] Christina Cogdell, 'The futurama recontextualized: Norman Bel Geddes's eugenic "world of tomorrow"', *American Quarterly* 52, 2 (2000), 195.

however, there was a constant tension between the forces of modernism and traditionalism when it came to food science. The company's commissary department gave careful attention to the safety of locally sourced food in Pan Am's outposts around the world. During the Second World War many food supplies were lost at sea, meaning that employees had to rely on local food, which was not trusted. Pan Am therefore established large company dining halls in African locations such as Lagos, Cairo and Khartoum, purchasing fruit and vegetables locally but then rigorously cleaning it before preparation in-house. By adding these African cities to its network, Pan Am had completed its worldwide chain of routes, taking control of them from the British Royal Air Force, a deal which was first agreed at a boozy London dinner between Trippe and British Prime Minister Winston Churchill in June 1941. In order to provide fresher and safer vegetables a five-acre farm was developed in Accra, where beans, carrots and tomatoes were grown. The company's medical staff in Africa, wary of employees contracting parasitic diseases, were charged with examining any meat purchased locally before it was prepared and served. Considering these safeguards sufficient they therefore did not supply supplementary vitamin capsules to staff. This was unusual for the time, particularly given Pan Am's embrace of modernism in other areas. Vitamins were discovered in the 1910s, but the Second World War proved a major catalyst in popularizing them in the United States, when the intertwining of nutrition and national defence saw vitamin sales more than double behind the alliterative slogan 'Vitamins for Victory!' In the belief that they improved productivity and cut down on absenteeism, fatigue and spoilage, many American businesses issued vitamin supplements to their workers en masse; the wartime vitamin distribution programmes in aviation companies such as Northrop and North American Aviation are particularly noteworthy.[17] However Pan Am's doctors, in this instance, reflected the scepticism of many established physicians and health officials towards the vitamin supplement craze as something driven by the commercial interests of the chemical industry. As one eminent nutritional scientist of the time put it, 'the crying need for better nutrition can be answered only with food. Giving synthetic vitamins is a stopgap procedure'.[18]

This primary scientific emphasis on food was echoed by the company's medical advisers, who cautioned staff deployed abroad against purchasing any

[17] Rima D. Apple, 'Vitamins win the war: Nutrition, commerce, and patriotism in the United States during the Second World War', in David F. Smith and Jim Phillips (eds), *Food, Science, Policy and Regulation in the Twentieth Century* (Abingdon: Routledge, 2000), 135–49.

[18] Wilbur A. Sawyer, cited in Apple, 'Vitamins', 143.

food 'from restaurants in cities like Cairo' to eat as in-flight snacks.[19] During the war Pan Am's medical department drew up a booklet on tropical health rules warning staff against 'green salads, uncooked fish, vegetables or other raw products', 'cream pies, cream fillings or fricasses' and 'any milk or ice cream derived from local sources'. Water derived locally had to be boiled and bottled water was not to be trusted unless it came from American sources. Alcohol was to be consumed only moderately. After one crew on an African route suffered near-deadly food poisoning the company's medical team insisted that from that point onwards all food consumed in-flight had to be prepared at company dining halls. Food safety and wartime security concerns were ensuring that the quaint charm of the purser shopping for delicacies from local markets during layovers was becoming a thing of the past. The company's medical team also issued the following instructions for crews following emergency sea landings: 'if you have water, don't eat'; 'don't drink liquor, save it for men who are severely wounded'; 'don't drink urine'; and 'for relief chew on untanned leather, cloth or buttons'.[20]

The airline meal: Freezing, heating and aluminium

The Second World War would also provide an important precedent when it came to refrigeration in food transit. Although commercial flight took second stage to the transport of war cargoes during the early 1940s, the science underpinning cargo transit would inspire later technologies, in particular the flash-freezing of meals (freezing food at extremely low temperatures with cold air). In 1945 Pan Am transported half a million fish eggs to Lake Titicaca, a gift from the US government to the government of Peru and intended to improve fish stocks in the famous lake. The fertilized eggs needed to be kept at a consistent low temperature, which required research in collaboration with the US government's Fisheries Department around how this could be achieved through ice packaging and refrigeration.[21] These experiments in in-flight freezing informed what was one of Pan Am's most significant but underestimated 'firsts': the mass distribution of frozen, pre-packaged airline food. As mentioned previously, this was the first

---

[19] 'The Cannonball: A history of America's Africa-Orient air lifeline', University of Miami special collections, Pan Am collection no. 341, series I, box 18, folder 7.

[20] 'The Cannonball: A history of America's Africa-Orient air lifeline', University of Miami special collections, Pan Am collection no. 341, series I, box 18, folder 7.

[21] 'The flying clippers of the Southern Americas' (1945), Pan Am collection no. 341, series I, box 64, folder 6.

appearance of the airline meal as we know it today, and therefore it bears more detailed consideration.

Mechanical refrigeration had come into wide use in the late nineteenth century and by the 1920s and 1930s quick freezing was used to preserve fish, most famously by the Birds Eye corporation.[22] However, the application of refrigeration to airline food was another matter. The first planes lacked kitchen facilities; without these, a hot meal needed to be pre-cooked or par-cooked and kept at temperature, which tended to break down delicate proteins and starches. These problems were overcome via on-board kitchens, which first appeared in the 1930s. It was the post-war period, though, where food technology started to improve markedly. When, in 1946, Pan Am became the first airline to introduce the now common method of basing in-flight service on pre-cooked frozen food, which preserved food and eliminated wastage, the meals themselves were cooked at the Maxson plant in Queens, New York. They were then flash-frozen at twenty degrees below zero, before storage in separate refrigerators at minus ten degrees. The food was then transported to the various Pan Am stations by land, sea or air and could be stored for several months if necessary. Pan Am located its main flight kitchens in New York and Paris and these functioned as central hubs where food was cooked, frozen and packaged for international distribution. This was the first example of the now standard international distribution of pre-packaged airline food in aluminium trays, a convenience which would be swiftly adopted by Pan Am's main competitors such as TWA and Qantas.[23]

Pan Am's decision to take this industry-changing step was outlined in a landmark memorandum of 1946 penned by company executive Melville Stone. The company could either reluctantly embrace frozen meals as a necessary evil, he wrote, or choose to distinguish their brand from foreign and domestic competition by unleashing a food service scientifically 'second to none', one which would embrace the newest technologies in freezing and heating food but also retain a focus on culinary excellence. Stone went on to explain how Pan Am had pioneered the serving of frozen food as early as 1939 with the food heated on galley steam tables, but in 1945 it began issuing contracts to inventor William Maxson who, as mentioned, had worked with the US government during the Second World War, providing oven units for military transports.[24] Post-war,

---

[22] For more on Birds Eye's innovations see Mark Kurlansky, *Birdseye: The Adventures of a Curious Man* (New York: Random House, 2012).

[23] Foss attributes this 'first' to TWA in 1947, but Pan Am's introduction of frozen food to overseas operations predated their competitor's by a year. See Foss, *Food in the Air and Space*, 66.

[24] Melville Stone memorandum, 5 December 1946, University of Miami digital collections, Pan Am material. Courtesy of Gabrielle Williams.

eyeing the civilian market, Maxson came up with the first multi-compartment plate oven and, thanks to its wartime activity, Pan Am was perfectly placed to collaborate with him. But while the linkage of Pan Am's experience in refrigeration and Maxson's experience in heating was to change airline food forever – announcing the arrival of the standard airline meal – the professional relationship was to prove short-lived, as outlined later.

These bold new moves also required the development of new food safety checks which by later standards appear rudimentary. In ensuring a quality and flavoursome product, the temperature at which a frozen product was held after freezing was important, since any variation in temperature caused damage. Therefore, just before departure, pursers were required to place the pre-packaged meals in a pre-chilled balsa wood chest covered with stainless steel, which kept the food frozen for up to forty-eight hours. The purser then had to periodically check that the food was sufficiently chilled by placing an ice cube in a small wire cage under the lid of the chest. If the ice cube was still intact after the chest was opened, the food was safe; if not, the contents were discarded.[25] Another factor in guaranteeing the palatability and safety of frozen food was packaging. For the purser, the advent of the aluminium tray may have resulted in more cuts to the hand, but it was also a blessing because it removed the necessity to wash up. Trays also provided compact storage, eliminating some of the weight and space problems encountered earlier in-flight meal service. From the perspective of management, the frozen meal perfectly accompanied the post-war expansion of the industry and the scheduling problems associated with an increase in the number of flights in the air; previously, when a flight was cancelled, the food that had been prepared was wasted, whereas now it could simply be used again.

More significantly, though, the use of aluminium also prevented the dehydration of the frozen product, which would have accelerated the loss of flavour and juiciness. Aluminium was already established as the metal used for aircraft themselves. Several governments, including that of the United States, had fuelled the global expansion of aluminium in the 1930s and 1940s, developing the industrial conversion of bauxite to aluminium, which in turn enabled the mass production of military aircraft during the Second World War. Post-war, aluminium became popular as a convenience product in the mass consumption of food, based around the ability of aluminium foil to bar light,

---

[25] Whyte, 'The early pursers: Chief cooks, bottlewashers, and in-flight typists'.

oxygen, moistness, odours, flavours and germs. In introducing the aluminium tray meal to airline dining, Pan Am anticipated the wider proliferation of 'TV dinners' in America in the 1960s: a convenience item enabled by the use of aluminium to make packaging that could be heated in the oven, served, and then easily disposed of post-meal. Single-use aluminium packaging would become symbolic of the 'throwaway society' of the United States, becoming an icon of US foodstuffs from Jiffy Pop popcorn to supermarket ready meals to the restaurant takeout meal.[26] It would not be long, too, before the aluminium soft drink can also became a fixture of airline meal service.

The ice cube check aside, the now-familiar aluminium tray airplane meal was subjected to food safety controls from the outset. All meals served in-flight were prepared on the ground to the specifications of appointed food consultants. To quote a company press release from 1946, when this new type of airline food service began, meals were pre-prepared 'under the strictest US sanitary conditions', thus ensuring 'the same high quality of food at all times'.[27] In 1945 Trippe had enlisted the advice of dieticians at the Cornell University College of Home Economics. At the time, the US food standards programme was among the best in the world. Early federal regulation, through the 1906 Pure Food and Drugs Act, led to the creation of the Food and Drug Administration in 1930 and historians generally agree that businesses, in turn, benefited from the resultant confidence and goodwill of consumers.[28] Companies like Pan Am could therefore point to their compliance with US food safety standards as a way of assuring customers. The aluminium tray airplane meal – consumed by passengers and crew in the knowledge that it had met American food safety standards – eliminated the health risks associated with the old practice of pursers purchasing and serving local food. As a corollary, and as discussed later, it also intensified the globalization of a quintessentially American culture of 'throwaway' food tastes and practices.

---

[26] Carl A. Zimring, *Aluminium Upcycled: Sustainable Design in Historical Perspective* (Baltimore, MD: John Hopkins University Press, 2017), 1–44. See also Mimi Sheller, *Aluminium Dreams: The Making of Light Modernity* (Cambridge, MA: MIT Press, 2014), 13. See also Harvey Levenstein, *Paradox of Plenty: A Social History of Eating in Modern America* (Oxford: Oxford University Press, 1993), 227–36.

[27] Jane Kilbourne, 'Clipper kitchens', *New Horizons*, April–June 1946. University of Miami special collections, Pan Am collection no. 341, series I, box 291, folder 4.

[28] Suzanne White Junod, 'Food standards in the United States: The case of the peanut butter and jelly sandwich', in David F. Smith and Jim Phillips (eds), *Food, Science, Policy and Regulation in the Twentieth Century* (Abingdon: Routledge, 2000), 167.

Standardization: Compatible with 'good food'?

In establishing the international norm of mass, safe, pre-packaged airline food, the company was also anticipating the global standardization of foodstuffs and, with it, the further globalization of the food trade. Although founded in 1948 and 1945, respectively, it was not until 1962 that the World Health Organization and the United Nations Food and Agriculture Organization introduced the *Codex Alimentarius*: a collection of internationally adopted scientific food standards. In the wake of the Geneva international conference on food standards at which the Codex was agreed upon, international bodies developed standard analytical methods for measuring, for example, the purity of additives in food.[29] Such strides in standardization were aimed at protecting consumer health and improving food safety in developing countries, as well as expanding international trade.[30] Pan Am was a corporate precursor to these trends. Its marketing around airline food in the post-war period emphasized the idea of the global-as-local, with food sourced locally, but – importantly – prepared in company kitchens to reliable (US) food standards. It stands as a good example of US Cold War exceptionalism: 'progressive', standardized globalization was taking place but only under US rules. The result was, to quote from Melville Stone's 1946 memorandum once more, the 'uniformity' and 'simplicity' of 'world-wide standardization' and the 'unquestioned sanitation' of airline food.[31]

Many of these advancements were thanks to the rotund and enigmatic frozen food enthusiast William Maxson. In the immediate post-war period, the partnership with the Maxson company guaranteed standardization. Using Maxson's latest oven technology to efficiently warm food overcame some of the problems encountered pre-war when, as mentioned, food and beverages were heated using liquid fuel stoves or steam chests and where alcohol was used as the chosen fuel. Cooking with alcohol may have been preferable to kerosene or butane (because it was less flammable, more lightweight and gave off less odour when cooking), but it also gave off much less heat and took much longer. The steam chest, similarly, was only capable of low temperatures. Channelling

---

[29] Survey of Analytical Methods Available for the Estimation of Food Additives in Food, 1970. Science History Institute, Philadelphia, Records of the International Union of Pure and Applied Chemistry, series XII, box 156 (Commission on Food Chemistry – 1).

[30] Report on the Food Standards Conference, 19 October 1962. Science History Institute, Philadelphia, Records of the International Union of Pure and Applied Chemistry, series XII, box 156 (Commission on Food Chemistry – 1).

[31] Melville Stone memorandum, 5 December 1946, University of Miami digital collections, Pan Am material. Courtesy of Gabrielle Williams.

the heat from the exhaust pipes of the plane's engine was also imperfect as it brought more engine noise and a cracked pipe would bring the engine's exhaust fumes into the cabin.[32] As early as 1939 Pan Am had established its leadership in the field by using electric fan-assisted ovens to heat roast beef aboard its Boeing 314 flying boat, but it took the first efficient convection ovens, those of William Maxson, to transform the mid-air warming of food through a reliable standard product. Now, in the air, food was heated in the state-of-the-art electric Whirlwind Oven, designed by Maxson himself. The Whirlwind enabled six meals to be prepared every fifteen minutes; this model was soon improved to a twelve-plate electric oven with thermostatic control and fan to ensure the even distribution of heat. Experts from the Maxson Corporation also designed the galleys for the Clipper fleet in the mid-1940s.[33] By the early 1950s, and the Stratocruiser, oven capacity had increased to twenty-four plates at a time and oven heat could reach 700 degrees Fahrenheit in seventeen minutes.[34] Reflecting increased passenger numbers, the capacity and efficiency of food preparation were improving.

An important reason for this improvement was the company's incorporation of food service as an integral part of its expanded system, and here we return to William Maxson. This meant, in turn, relying less on subcontractors and expanding every aspect of its food operations. While recognizing Maxson's ingenuity in perfecting ovens, Pan Am executive Melville Stone was less than complementary about the man himself, attributing his 'lust for food' to his weight (over 300 lb) and his lack of a housewife following his divorce: his 'home domestic problem' explained his original experiments with oven cooking, claimed Stone. Stone's sniffy attitude towards the corpulent Maxson was pre-echoed by the *New Yorker* magazine, which sent a reporter to dinner with the man in August 1945. As well as caricaturing him as a left-handed Henry VIII, the *New Yorker*'s profile cast Maxson as something of an oddball neophile:

We dined with Mister Maxson in his office, which is air conditioned, has a kitchen, and overlooks the Hudson. In addition to defrosted ham steak platter, we had defrosted hors d'oeuvre, defrosted bread and butter, defrosted coffee, defrosted after-dinner mints, and a defrosted Corona … 'it depends on the way you do it, and the way I do it is special' Mister Maxson told us. 'Take the hors

---

[32] Foss, *Food in the Air and Space*, 31–2.
[33] *New Horizons*, April–June 1946, University of Miami special collections, Pan Am collection no. 341, series I, box 291, folder 10.
[34] 'Welcome aboard your Clipper', University of Miami special collections, Pan Am collection no. 341, series I, box 108, folder 14.

d'oeuvre, for instance. I freeze the bread first. Then I put on cream cheese mixed with minced scallions, or just salami, and freeze it again. That keeps the bread from going soggy'.

As the dinner continued, the correspondent's bemusement grew:

The dinner we ate was defrosted in a metal box, called a Maxson's Whirlwind, through which hot air is blown. This process made a terrific racket. Mister Maxson explained that this was because he was using the twenty-four volt DC motor, that comes with the standard unit now used in airplanes.

Maxson went on to detail how his product, once provided exclusively to the Army and Navy, was now attracting commercial interest from the aviation industry. As he explained the process through which it went, the *New Yorker*'s reporter took notes:

'I guess they were impressed by the way we saved the Navy from SPAM' Maxson rather cattily remarked … the plates go through ovens on a conveyor belt … the cooked food is placed on cardboard treated with a coating of phenolic resin plastic. A cardboard disc is placed on top of the dish and sealed to it with a ring of plastic, and the meal is then kept at twenty below zero for four hours, by which time it's hard as yesterday's dinner rolls and in a state to last until Doomsday.

The *New Yorker*'s reference to Doomsday was badly timed for Maxson: the piece was published in exactly the same week that the atomic bomb was dropped on Hiroshima. In linking Maxson's innovation with the apocalypse threatened by the new atomic age, the *New Yorker* was decidedly turning its nose up at him. The piece concluded with a paragraph mocking Maxson's inspiration for his invention:

Maxson told us he got the idea of frozen dinners several years ago when he grew a surplus of cauliflower on his place in Jersey. He cooked and froze a little (for some reason) and upon tasting it a year later (for some reason) found that it was delicious. Now he never touches fresh food at home except for an occasional salad. His dinner guests are taken to the freezer and allowed to take out just what they'd like; one may take egg foo-young, another oyster stew, another curried chicken, and so on. None of this nonsense of everybody at the table eating the same thing.[35]

---

[35] 'Defrosted dinners', *The New Yorker*, 4 August 1945.

It is likely that Pan Am's Melville Stone read the *New Yorker* piece and decided to investigate further. He was received by the man himself in his premises overlooking the Hudson. Maxson, wrote Stone after touring his factory, would order frozen vegetables in bulk from Birds Eye, defrost them, cook them and freeze them again, before sending them on to Pan Am as part of a meal, which would be wrapped in plastic on a paper plate. This lengthy industrial process made for high prices and poor quality food, as the article implied. Although Pan Am's use of Maxson ovens would continue, Stone recommended ditching the company's reliance on Maxson for the food itself, highlighting the high price and poor quality of its processed product. He saw William Maxson's obesity as the embodiment of his company's unhealthy and overly processed approach to food and recommended that Trippe end the company's reliance on Maxson and his 'bunch of engineers trying to do a cooking job'. This advice was to usher in the attention to culinary detail for which Pan Am would gain renown. It was also Stone who foresaw the model kitchen and galley used at the company's training centre as a mandatory part of culinary training and he who recommended consulting the professionals via a Pan Am 'World Wide Committee of Chefs' to advise and innovate.[36] As if to prove Stone's point, Maxson's obesity would contribute to his death at the relatively young age of 58, in 1947, just months after Stone had composed his influential memo, and leading to the abrupt demise of his once mighty company. Maxson's pioneering methods, however, would live on.

Fresh

Melville Stone's focus on the quality of airline food spoke to the fact that in establishing the pre-packaged airline meal as the industry norm, the company faced a perhaps greater challenge: convincing passengers that it was fresh. Although freshness is one of the most desirable food qualities, to this day the very notion of what exactly 'fresh food' means is disputed, going beyond simple biological explanations and into the realm of cultural expectations. Throughout history, eating fresh food was a marker of wealth and status, something integral to the elitism of the Pan Am brand. In the twentieth century, moreover, the ability to consume fresh food connoted progress: countries whose people

---

[36] Melville Stone memorandum, 5 December 1946, University of Miami digital collections, Pan Am material. Courtesy of Gabrielle Williams.

enjoyed mass, affordable fresh food did so through advances in refrigeration.[37] Consequently, as an airline with both elite and progressive aspirations, Pan Am advertising often boasted of its 'fresh' food. By the mid-twentieth century, though, refrigeration had redefined what fresh meant. Given Stone's post-war decision that the company would take on most aspects of food preparation and distribution itself, just how fresh was Pan Am's fare?

It is generally agreed that foods frozen quickly are of better quality than foods frozen slowly because when foods are allowed to freeze slowly water molecules in the food have time to form larger ice crystals. Within Pan Am, much of the responsibility for ensuring fresh frozen food fell to the nautically titled 'port stewards' of the commissary department, who were located on the ground at the major airports. The port steward conveyed foodstuffs to be prepared and frozen rapidly, managing the ordering, distribution and stocking of food, drink, cutlery and crockery for flights, and driving trucks from the kitchens along the runway to load the waiting planes. A former port steward at San Francisco testified to how fresh the food was before it reached the kitchens. Fruit and vegetables would be delivered every morning from 'the fruit basket' in the nearby valley area, the fertile part of California symbolic of the association between fresh fruit and gorgeous youth.[38] Once at the airport it was rapidly offloaded, prepared in the company's kitchens, and – within eight to ten hours – packaged and frozen before being sent to destinations all over the world.[39] By modern standards, this was indeed fresh food. That it was served by nubile young women only enhanced the overall impression of 'freshness'.

The company also credited its scientists with enabling the service of fresh coffee in the air. Up until this point, coffee was usually made on the ground and served mid-flight from a thermos flask, which often resulted in the coffee cooling, especially on long trips. To passengers in early aircraft, which were unheated, a warming cup of coffee or tea was a welcome beverage, even if it came lukewarm from a thermos. In the 1930s, before electricity was used in-flight, engineers experimented with heating coffee mid-air using liquid fuel stoves and steam chests, but with limited and sporadic success.[40] After the Second World War and working in collaboration with the Krukin company of New Jersey, Pan Am devised a new type of coffee urn. The urn evolved from disagreements between the company's Atlantic and Pacific branches. Pacific claimed that since

[37] Susanne Freidberg, *Fresh: A Perishable History* (Cambridge, MA: Belknap, 2009), 1–8.
[38] Freidberg, *Fresh*, 125.
[39] Interview with Ed Nolan, 31 May 2018.
[40] Foss, *Food in the Air and Space*, 32.

Figure 2.2 Pan Am's post-war coffee urn. Courtesy: Foynes Flying Boat and Maritime Museum.

water boils at a lower temperature at altitude a pressurized urn was needed. Atlantic said that this wasn't necessary since coffee tasted just as good when it boiled at a lower temperature in the air. The company commissioned coffee tasters to investigate and they sided with the Atlantic division. An unpressurized coffee urn, from which coffee was served hot and freshly boiled, was therefore introduced to all Pan Am aircraft (Figure 2.2). The improved quality of the cup of coffee met with much acclaim. It tasted 'fresher', feedback claimed.[41]

If scientific innovation had enhanced the in-flight quality of that American staple – coffee – the accompanying sweet food was also subject to new techniques in food preservation. Solid carbon dioxide (dry ice) was first used commercially in the 1930s, quickly becoming popular in restaurants for its theatrical effect. Dry ice was first used by Pan Am in preserving food bound for the Pacific atolls it colonized, but soon it would become integral to 'Cherries Jubilee', a Pan Am dessert staple involving ice cream kept in dry ice (known, inimitably, to airline staff as the 'ice cream bomb') and topped with cherries heated in the oven.

[41] 'Mile-High Kitchen' (1950), University of Miami special collections, Pan Am collection no. 341, series I, box 108, folder 3.

Timing, naturally, was of the essence, with crew having to judge the correct time to remove the ice cream from the 'bomb' so that it would not melt too quickly.[42] Training staff in timing food preparation correctly was, in fact, long established. As early as 1937 laboratory tests conducted at the company's scientific facilities in California had determined that a 'three-minute egg' was actually a three-and-a-half-minute egg at 5,000 feet and a four-and-a-half-minute egg at 12,000 feet.[43] Building provisioning around food science also came into play. Not enough dry ice and the frozen desserts could not be kept chilled and in serving condition; too much dry ice on a serving tray and the salad would start to freeze.

As discussed later, the theatrical choice of centrepiece dessert again demonstrated the high dining ambitions of the company: Cherries Jubilee is credited to French master chef Auguste Escoffier, who is said to have developed the dish for Queen Victoria's 1897 jubilee. The flaming liqueur also bears a strong similarity to another of Escoffier's creations from his time at London's Savoy Hotel, a flaming ice called the *Bombe Néro*. Eventually the practice of preparing Cherries Jubilee – with dry ice added to crème de menthe, appearing to produce smoke – had to be stopped due to nervous passengers thinking there was a fire on board the airplane.[44] Parenthetically, the fear of fire hazard also stymied some of Pan Am's rivals in their attempts to reconstruct authentically national dishes mid-air. Swissair, for example, planned to prepare cheese fondue in the traditional manner but decided that cooking it in front of passengers using a naked flame was too much of a safety risk, especially when going through air pockets.[45] By the 1960s, looking over its shoulder at this sort of authentically national cuisine offered by an increasingly busy field of international rivals, Pan Am was further impelled towards culinary transnationalism.

A Brave New World on earth and in space

There was something about the smoking, flaming theatricality of the 'ice cream bomb' which imbued the airborne food server with the extravagant air of the experimental laboratory scientist. This spoke to the self-image of the company, which was based around the idea that it occupied the vanguard

[42] Interview with Barrie Fewster, 23 January 2018.
[43] 'What's a three minute egg?', *Pan American Air Ways*, vol. 8, no. 10, November 1937, p. 2. University of Miami digital collections, Pan Am material.
[44] Interview with Harry Frahm, 15 March 2018.
[45] 'Dining Up', *The New Yorker*, 22 July 1961.

of the march of scientific progress. As Juan Trippe himself put it, Pan Am's system was a 'working laboratory' continuously searching for the next 'revolutionary advancement'.[46] His company's expansion into Alaska and the Arctic regions had come early, in the 1930s; these were not profitable routes, the company acknowledged, but the Arctic was viewed as a 'laboratory', a place for 'experimental' initiatives.[47] In-house publications from the 1950s reiterated how Pan Am had been at the cutting edge of new techniques in food production (notably hydroponics in the Pacific) and now looked towards the untapped potential of the polar regions. While Arctic conditions were not conducive to the cultivation of cereals and vegetables, staff were informed, the grasslands of the region provided resources such as meat, hides and other animal products.[48] In what would become a constant theme of its Cold War-era collaboration with the US government, Pan Am – which operated Arctic routes but desired more bases there – was flagging its potential not only as a tool of imperial expansion to the US government but also as a force for civilizational improvement for the entire world.

A company propaganda pamphlet of 1944 entitled *A Forum of the Future* came complete with illustrations that would not have looked out of place in literature produced by fringe religious groups or the Soviet socialist realist school, picturing earnest men, women and children with eyes cast determinedly upwards to the heavens. Featuring contributions on the shape of the post-war world from scientists and explorers, the ability of aviation to deliver adequate food resources loomed large. President of the Massachusetts Institute of Technology, the physicist Karl Compton, was a contributor to *Forum of the Future*, writing that 'new appetizing food products, containing all essential ingredients for health and strength, will be packaged for easy distribution and storage and available at such low price as practically to eliminate under-nourishment'. The famous Icelandic-American explorer Vilhjalmur Stefansson was similarly upbeat. 'Man's path of progress leads north', he wrote, 'chief among mankind's needs is *food* – and the Arctic has untapped food resources in abundance!'[49]

[46] Carl B. Allen, notes of interview with Juan Trippe, undated, Carl B. Allen papers, box 8, folder 7, WVRAC.
[47] 'History of Pan American World Airways' (1946), University of Miami special collections, Pan Am collection no. 341, series I, box 196, folder 10.
[48] Pan American World Airways Teacher, vol. XIV, no. 1 (October 1957). University of Miami special collections, Pan Am collection no. 341, series I, box 62, folder 2.
[49] Pan American World Airways, *A Forum of the Future* (1944), Truman Library, George C. Neal papers, Pan American Airways file, box 26–9.

The company's frontier spirit was fitting to the age. As part of the Cold War Space Race of the 1950s, the US government conducted tests around the consumption of food and the human metabolism in space, illuminating how high altitude negatively effects taste and flavour. Many of these studies also pointed to a fundamental point – the consumption of food helped reduce stress and the mimicking of meals and mealtimes on earth brought great emotional and psychological satisfaction to humans experiencing airborne discomfort. One early American spaceman recalled nibbling on a small bag of salted nuts as his experimental capsule hurtled back to earth through a thunderstorm, his oxygen levels becoming dangerously low. 'The psychology here would be quite comparable to that of the frustrated, overweight housewife,' he later wrote, 'who munches on titbits of chocolate as a means of consolation.'[50] Pan Am's closeness to the US government's space programme was signalled by its Guided Missile Range Division (GMRD), created in 1953, which was renamed the Aerospace Services Division in 1967 and which serviced every major US space programme up until the 1980s. Functioning as part of what President Dwight D. Eisenhower termed the 'military-industrial complex', Pan Am's GMRD employees carried out a range of tasks for the US Air Force, from the storage of explosives to food preparation.[51]

The fact that Pan Am, a civilian company, was brought in to assist with a military programme is another example of the blurring of the lines when it came to its status: Was it a solely private enterprise or an instrument of state? At the same time, the company was just one of many US brands scrambling to associate with America's early space exploration. Prior to Soviet astronaut Yuri Gagarin's consumption of paste from tubes in 1961, a feat replicated by the United States' John Glenn on his orbit of earth in 1962, it was not even established that humans could eat and drink in space without vomiting it back up. NASA's early enquiries into food that could be consumed in weightless conditions built on techniques learned from the airline industry such as dehydrating and freeze-drying of foodstuffs. Although, in their most basic forms, these were ancient technologies, as one historian puts it, 'the Americans were obsessed with developing food as modern and ground-breaking as the program itself'.[52] Accordingly, in pursuing a new imperium in space, NASA looked to the airline industry and its scientific developments around food.

[50] Nadia Berenstein, 'Eating at 100,000 feet: Man high and the origins of space food', 8 March 2018. www.nadiaberenstein.com (accessed 12 June 2018).
[51] Van Vleck, *Empire of the Air*, 209.
[52] Foss, *Food in the Air and Space*, 159.

Green Eggs and Ham: The challenges of dining at altitude

In keeping with the scientific promise of the space age, aircraft were reaching higher scientific heights, too, with the dawn of higher altitude jet flight and the roll-out of the Boeing 707. Accompanying publicity emphasized the 'serenity' that came with that great selling point of the jet age: the lack of vibration. Passengers could now eat in comfort, served from 'four up-to-the-minute galleys, each equipped with the latest infra-red heating units'; the wines accompanying food service 'have never tasted better than they do eight miles above the earth in the satin smoothness of jet flight'.[53] Yet despite the fact that Pan Am placed a premium on *service*, technical deficiencies still militated against the experience of a good meal in the air. The earliest 707s were noisy and it was not until engine manufacturers began replacing turbojets with turbofans in the mid-1960s that jetliner noise was reduced.[54] Similarly, as alluded to previously, the 707 brought with it pressurized cabins, numbing taste buds as planes reached higher altitudes, and low cabin humidity, which weakened the sense of smell.

Some under-appreciated aspects of Pan Am's food service therefore demand consideration. Eating warm nuts – a staple of the Pan Am service often ignored as a preliminary to the main event – was as much about the calming psychological ritual of munching, as testified by the early astronauts, as it was about culinary satisfaction. Salt, too, was a vital and often overlooked accompaniment to airline food since sodium chloride is a taste molecule and its addition to in-flight meals did not merely bring saltiness, it also added flavour. Nonetheless, higher temperature mid-flight, when combined with low humidity, could have undesirable effects on efforts to create earthly meals at altitude. These problems were identified as early as the 1930s; at the time, aircraft still flew at relatively low altitude but if they had to climb (to overcome mountains, for instance) it was noted that it took longer to boil an egg, milk would curdle and freshly baked rolls became dry very quickly.[55] Former flight attendant Helen Davey recalled how the altitude meant that omelettes had a tendency to turn green if overcooked for just one minute – 'a putrid, nauseating green'.[56] Many a former Pan Am flight attendant has an 'egg story'. One attendant working the first-class galley on a 707 outbound from Singapore and Guam to Honolulu and preparing for breakfast service before the sun came up recalled:

---

[53] Pan Am promotional brochure, '707 Jet Clippers' (1958, courtesy of Becky Sprecher).
[54] Sutter, *747: Creating the World's First Jumbo Jet and Other Adventures from a Life in Aviation*, 70.
[55] Foss, *Food in the Air and Space*, 75.
[56] Helen Davey, '350 Eggs but who's counting?', *Huffington Post*, 17 July 2011.

a nice man appeared and in a genteel Southern drawl, asked for something to drink. Being from the South, we struck up a conversation. He asked to see the galley, and I showed him everything. We shook hands and I introduced myself, Then he said in a very unassuming manner that he was Craig Claiborne, food editor of the *New York Times*. God in heaven! I grew pale – I'm certain of it. Then I glanced at the order sheet clipped to the galley wall. He'd ordered eggs over easy. So I just fessed up, and said, 'Oh Mr. Claiborne! I had no idea of who you were! I'm afraid I'm going to have to fix you eggs in a few hours, I'll overcook them, they'll be green.' He laughed gently, and patting my arm said, 'That will be fine, Becky. Not to worry.' Then he turned and went back to his seat.[57]

Clearly, when faced with the unappetizing prospect of green eggs, even the *New York Times* food critic sympathized with the scientific challenges attached to cooking at altitude. However, some of these challenges were to be overcome through science and engineering. The introduction of the 747 was accompanied by strides in food technology. It was equipped with the latest convection ovens, which were not widely commercially available in America at the time. The new jets also made some limited use of the microwave oven, an invention which promised to make cooking easier and quicker but was generally not used mid-air because of the fire risk and its small size. On the ground, the food was loaded straight into the galley via a newly designed mobile unit, which locked into a loading hatch beneath the plane. This enabled food to be kept under constant refrigeration from ground kitchen to aircraft.[58] This galley in the aircraft's belly was then elevated up to passenger level ready for service, ensuring passengers were spared much of the manual spectacle of the loading. The system was in fact a Russian innovation but one which, in typical imperialistic spirit, Pan Am claimed as its own. Serving 362 people aboard the 747 necessitated a staggering 10,000 pieces of silver and dishes and glasses per flight (1,200 glasses, 5,720 items of chinaware and trays, and 3,230 knives, forks and spoons). The new 'plug-in' galley meant that after a flight all the waste food and dirty dining items were removed as one – as part of the galley unit – and replaced by a new mobile galley unit within twenty minutes.[59]

Flight attendants on the 747, trained in food hygiene and safety, carried meat thermometers so that signature dishes like the chateaubriand were served at

[57] Interview with Becky Sprecher, 24 January 2018.
[58] Eric Burgess, 'Dining on the jumbos', *Christian Science Monitor*, 8 January 1970. Pan Am collection no. 341, series I, box 111, folder 2.
[59] 'Pan Am's 747' (1970), University of Miami special collections, Pan Am collection no. 341, series I, box 65, folder 7.

the correct and safe temperature.[60] Scientifically, beef was a perfect centrepiece dish because, unlike other foods, fresh is not best with beef; instead the meat self-tenderizes over time, with the ageing (or rotting) process concentrating the flavour.[61] Keeping the vegetables accompanying the chateaubriand warm was a challenge so a bain-marie (heated water can) was used. Other small innovations to make food service more efficient would become a standard feature of air travel in the jet age. For example, passengers remembering the motherly adage of always washing one's hand before eating would often disrupt service by visiting the bathroom just prior to their food arriving; returning after service, they would then cause their neighbours to have to get up mid-meal, tray in hand, and walk into the aisle to enable them to get back to their seats. This problem was overcome by the policy of handing out hot wet towels prior to meal service:[62] something consistent with the Old World tradition of using finger bowls for washing hands.

In the latter decades of its operation, food safety would increasingly become a matter of attention for Pan Am because of the need to conform to international standards and the public's heightened awareness of food standards. For example, the insecticide sprayed into the cabin on the inaugural Pan Am flight was now a distant memory as all airlines had to comply with World Health Organization-approved in-flight vapour disinfection methods.[63] With increased customer awareness about diet and nutrition, compliance with the food safety standards of international bodies and the American Food and Drug Administration became priority. This included the cleaning of aircraft. In 1988 the company found itself in hot water with the US Department of Agriculture after inspections revealed many empty milk cartons stuffed down the sides and in the seat-back pockets of inbound international flights.[64] In 1987, a number of customer complaints related to the erosion of styrofoam cups when tea with hot lemon was served, with passengers fearing that they were damaging their health by consuming styrene. This query led to Pan Am's director of cabin supplies to issue staff with a notice from the Society of the Plastics Industry Inc. assuring them that citrus oils when combined with hot water indeed resulted in the pitting of cups, but that no actual styrene was released during the process and there was therefore

[60] Email correspondence with Barbara Sharfstein, 15 January 2018.
[61] Freidberg, *Fresh*, 50.
[62] Frahm, *Above and Below the Clouds*, 158.
[63] Erica Sheward, *Aviation Food Safety* (Oxford: Blackwell, 2006), 265.
[64] Pan Am Monthly operational bulletin, vol. 18, no. 5, June 1988, University of Miami Libraries digital collections, Pan Am material.

no hazard to human health.[65] But while Pan Am continued to pride itself on its food standards, the increasingly competitive environment of the 1980s meant that proportionately less resources were allocated to research and development than in previous decades. This marked a departure for the company since, when it came to the science attached to in-flight dining, Pan Am had pioneered many of the techniques and processes that later became industry norms. On the other hand, and as discussed in the following chapter, the perception of dining well in-flight always was, and remains, only partially attributable to science.

---

[65]   Pan Am Monthly operational bulletin, vol. 17, no. 9, June 1987, University of Miami Libraries digital collections, Pan Am material.

3

High dining: The indulgent embrace of the restaurant in the air

Introducing the French Connection

The term 'gastronomy' – the study of food and culture – first came into common usage in France, the country most associated with the notion of fine dining. By contrast, the American embrace of gastronomy as a concept came late. It was not until the 1910s that the health pitfalls of gulping down a heavy calorific, meaty, greasy diet underwent sustained attack at the hands of American food reformers like Henry Theophilus Finck, who lamented that his countrymen seemed immune to the pleasures of the table. Finck was writing at a time when the industrial production and consumption of processed food was exciting fears about its deleterious effect on the American nation. His was a view shared by contemporaries from Kellogg's founder John Harvey Kellogg – who believed that the consumption of grain-based cereals as a breakfast staple would help curb the impulse to masturbate – to Horace Fletcher, 'the great masticator', who advocated the prolonged chewing of food in order to extract the maximum nutritional benefits. Finck would write of the potential of a new "Gastronomic America" where the ordinary man or woman could properly enjoy a healthy meal via a less industrialized food chain that embraced local produce. Civilizational improvement was at the heart of Finck's message. A 'civilized meal' should be available to 'the humblest tiller of the soil or railway employee', not just to 'those who can cross the ocean and pay for Parisian dainties'.[1]

Partly due to such geographical and historical factors, and as with the notion of gastronomy, the American public came to embrace French cuisine relatively

---

[1] Henry Theophilus Finck, cited in Nadia Berenstein, 'The man who shook the United States by its taste buds', *Aeon*, 17 December 2017. Accessible via www.nadiaberenstein.com (accessed 12 June 2018).

belatedly. While the American upper classes had embraced many of the features of French dining by the late nineteenth century and French influence could be seen in popular Victorian home cookbooks, it has been claimed that the mass shift towards French food came as late as the publication of the book *Mastering the Art of French Cooking*, co-authored by celebrity chef and American housewives' favorite Julia Child, in 1961. Following good sales, Child was commissioned to star in one of the best-known cookery shows broadcast on US television, *The French Chef*. Following her death in 2004, the American nation's debt to Julia Child was established through the permanent exhibition of her kitchen at the National Museum of American History (the Smithsonian). One historian argues that Child's book and television series did more than any other event in the last half-century to reshape the gourmet dining scenery in the United States.[2] And yet these trends were preceded by Pan Am's embrace of Gallic cuisine and culture, which came at least a decade earlier.

This embrace came in the form of Pan Am's partnership with the acclaimed Maxim's restaurant on Paris's Rue Royale, which began in 1952. In the flying boat days, as mentioned, food service was generally restricted to cold buffet foods: better suited to the shorter range, daytime island-hopping service that Pan Am provided in the Caribbean. With the advent of transatlantic air travel, though, 'Parisian dainties' were closer than ever before. The gastronomic possibilities that air travel presented were made apparent to the Trippes on a visit to Paris in 1936. The city's restaurants and bistros were to the liking of the couple, who were hosted by Air France officials and enjoyed a convivial time, charmed by heavily accented discussions of world affairs over fine food and fine wine. It was on this occasion that the Trippes first dined at the renowned Maxim's, Betty Trippe recording in her diary that it was 'very crowded but very gay'.[3] Fast forward two decades, and a generation of Pan Am flight attendants would learn how to heat the Maxim's de Paris Coq au Vin to just the right temperature.

Transatlantic routes were always Trippe's dream because they were the most financially lucrative air linkage in the world. Thus, the development of the President's Special menu (1948) was not only a prominent symbol of the blending of Old World sophistication and New World progressiveness but also a shot across the bows of Pan Am's major international competitors

---

[2] David Strauss, *Setting the Table for Julia Child: Gourmet Dining in America, 1934–1961* (Baltimore: Johns Hopkins University Press, 2011), 221.
[3] Trippe, *The Diary and Letters*, 83.

Figure 3.1 In the early days of the partnership, Pan Am executives visit the kitchens of Maxim's, Paris. Courtesy: Ed Nolan.

KLM, Air France and British Overseas Airways Corporation (BOAC). The warning was duly received, but the President's Special still felt, and sounded, very American. In the course of competition with the world's other major airlines, cultural capital was assuming ever greater importance. Therefore when Trippe, in 1952, offered an exclusive contract to a satellite company of Maxim's (Société d'Achats Directs d'Alimentation) he was really laying down the gauntlet to the big European airlines: Pan Am was capable of Parisian culinary sophistication. Thereafter, Maxim's would supply frozen food to Pan Am for all classes of passenger and its logo would distinguish Pan Am's menus. It was a relationship which would last until 1971 and would cement Trippe's company's reputation for gastronomic excellence.[4] As this chapter outlines, it was also a new departure: Pan Am was accumulating greater cultural capital by appropriating Old World authenticity and repackaging it as a new, transnational offering (Figure 3.1).

---

[4] Dian Stirn Groh with Becky Snider Sprecher, 'Parisian partnership: Pan Am and Maxim's', *Jet Wings* (Winter/Spring 2016).

Airship to airplane: Could the restaurant experience be recreated in the air?

Prior to a full discussion of the French partnership, which elevated the panache of dining Pan Am to new cultural heights, the logistics enabling the transformation of high dining bear consideration. The notion of luxury dining in the skies dated back to the airship era before the First World War, when Zeppelin passengers enjoyed food catered by restaurants and loaded before departure, served with champagne on tables decorated with white linen and china. In 1935 Captain C. E. Rosendahl of the US Navy delivered a radio lecture in which he highlighted the benefits of the airship over the airplane. One of Rosendahl's main points was the smoother motion of the airship; in contrast to the plane, he claimed, even the roughest flying conditions had failed to induce air sickness aboard the airship. And whereas the space on airplanes was restricted, passengers on airships had 'abundant room for moving about, spacious dining rooms, lounging rooms, smoking rooms, as well as promenade decks ... a bar and even a piano.'[5] Although the lack of heating aboard airships hampered the luxury of eating in one, the leading airship of the post-war era, the Hindenburg, did indeed feature table service, complete with piano and cocktail bar.[6] Quite simply, because of their size, eating aboard an airship felt much more like being in a restaurant than eating on a plane did.

In May 1936 the Hindenburg, decorated with Nazi insignia, completed its first voyage to the United States, arriving at New Jersey after a record-breaking sixty-one-and-a-half-hour trip. The US press breathlessly reported on the size of the craft, approvingly noting the large cargo capacity enabling it to carry over a thousand pounds of foodstuffs for its passengers: four cases of American rye whisky; 150 quarts of German beer; a 'liberal' supply of pumpernickel; half a dozen bunches of bananas; several crates of pineapples, grapefruit, oranges, potatoes, spinach and lettuce; fresh refrigerated meat, including a crate of dressed turkeys; a barrel of live lobsters; and numerous cases of mineral water and ginger ale.[7] Following the successful trip, a pamphlet produced by the Goodyear tyre and rubber company entitled 'Why Doesn't America Have Airships?' placed

---

[5] C. E. Rosendahl, 'Airships', transcript of radio broadcast, 26 December 1935. Carl B. Allen papers, box 3, folder 2, WVRAC.

[6] See Harold Dick and Douglas Robinson, *Golden Age of the Great Passenger Airships* (Washington DC: Smithsonian Press, 1985).

[7] Carl B. Allen, 'Hindenburg set to return to Germany', *New York Herald Tribune*, 12 May 1936. Carl B. Allen papers, box 8, folder 3, WVRAC.

food central to the argument, recalling the use of its blimps to deliver food aid to an icebound village in Chesapeake Bay and describing the cuisine on board the Hindenburg as 'comparable to the best in this country or abroad'. 'In short', the Goodyear pamphlet argued, 'the airship achieves the advantage of a much swifter mode of travel without sacrificing those features of an ocean voyage which make it a *pleasant* experience.' Dining on board an airship was 'like that on a luxurious passenger train' whereas eating on a plane could be 'compared with the motor car'.[8]

In the competition between the two types of airborne travel, the spectacular destruction of the Hindenburg in 1937 would do much to secure the airplane's supremacy.[9] The most significant factor, though, was speed. In the 1930s debates raged in America between what aviation journalist Carl B. Allen termed 'the airplane crowd' and 'the airship crowd'. Airships were a better established and safer form of intercontinental transport whose champions pointed to the still-experimental nature of plane travel across large distances and the greater risks involved. But what gave the 'airplane crowd' legitimacy in their 'sublime contempt' for the 'airship crowd', wrote Allen, was the fact that, relatively speaking, the airship was an 'airborne tortoise'.[10] Allen was one of the exclusive band of five newsmen who made the first trans-Pacific flight with Pan Am in 1936 and ever after was something of an evangelist for the transnational, cutting-edge modernity that the company represented. Even so, the quote illustrates the furious pace of airborne development: in June 1936, Allen had reported enthusiastically on how Hindenburg, on its third trip to America, had outstripped the fastest steamship in the world – Queen Mary – by a comfortable two and a half days despite having travelled six hundred extra miles.[11] However, given their large surface area and greater drag force the airships were much slower than the newest planes, at their peak taking two or three days to cross the Atlantic. This may have made dining more leisurely, more restaurant like, but by contrast the greatly reduced transit times provided by Pan Am's early expansion facilitated the development of previously unthinkable menus which were fresher and more exciting. This impacted the world of fine dining not just in the air

8 Goodyear, 'Why Doesn't America Have Airships?' (1936). Carl B. Allen papers, box 3, folder 2, WVRAC.
9 For greater context on the aeroplane/airship battle see Alexander Rose, *Empires of the Sky: Zeppelins, Airplanes, and Two Men's Epic Duel to Rule the World* (New York: Penguin, 2020).
10 Carl B. Allen, notes on aeroplanes versus airships (undated, c.1934–7). Carl B. Allen papers, box 3, folder 2, WVRAC.
11 Carl B. Allen, '3rd trip to US breaks record of Hindenburg', *New York Herald Tribune*, 23 June 1936. Carl B. Allen papers, box 8, folder 3, WVRAC.

but on the ground, a good example being the transport of seafood. As Pan Am pushed ever more vigorously into Latin America, the company emphasized high society epicures settling down to lunch in the fine restaurants of Buenos Aires could now sample Pacific lobsters, renowned for their size and flavour, delivered fresh that morning from the coast of Chile, on the opposite side of the continent.[12]

Similarly, company publicity contained yarns about how the speed of airplane travel guaranteed *fresh* food, such as the following story from 1955:

BRESCIA RESTAURANT OWNER GOES TO FISH MARKET WITH PRIVATE PLANE

Ottorino, owner of the prestigious Igea restaurant, Viale de Stazione in Brescia, northern Italy, has been nicknamed the "flying caterer". Every morning he takes off in his private plane from Brescia and goes shopping on the fish markets on the Tyrrhenian and Adriatic seas, returning to Brescia in time for preparing his now famous fish recipes.[13]

Whether true or not, the association of airplane travel and diversely sourced fresh food sounded loud and clear. Pan Am's championing of fresh fish pre-echoes more recent consumer demand for fresh food – rather than canned, cured or frozen – and expanded the possibilities for fresh produce well beyond the immediately local. Sampling Parisian dainties in Paris may have still been largely an elite preserve, but the post-war democratization of air travel was starting to change this. Juan Trippe would replicate Finck's message of civilizational improvement for all but would expand the idea of accessible fresh produce from the local to the global, claiming that aviation 'has become a vital link between the new world and the old'.[14] Regional and national barriers would be collapsed. Like Finck, Trippe wanted the civilized meal to be available to the average American; unlike Finck, he wanted him to be able to cross the ocean and sample Parisian dainties to boot. In doing so, the logistical capabilities of jet flight combined with the technique of flash-freezing and rapid heating acted as his vehicle; Maxim's, in reality, was little more than Trippe's façade. But what a façade it was!

---

[12] 'The flying clippers of the Southern Americas' (1945), Pan Am collection no. 341, series I, box 64, folder 6.

[13] 'Tourist news from Italy', September 1955, Truman Library, Edward H. Foley papers, Pan American World Airways file, box 25.

[14] Juan Trippe, 'Ocean air transport', 29th Wilbur Wright Memorial Lecture, 17 June 1941. Truman Library, George C. Neal papers, Pan American Airways file, box 26–8.

Maxim's

Maxim's was founded in 1893 by former waiter Maxime Gaillard and remains a feature of central Paris. The restaurant quickly gained fame for its distinctive art nouveau decor and stylish exterior. Completed in time for the Paris World's Fair in 1900, Maxim's exterior features a distinctive crimson awning with bold gold art deco lettering, rich dark wood panels and huge plate glass windows; inside, ambient lighting illuminates images of fauna, flora and feminine charm in the art nouveau style. However, the owner of the restaurant during the belle époque, Eugène Cornuché, claimed that its secret weapon was in fact beautiful women, claiming 'an empty room … never! I always have a beauty sitting by the window, in view from the sidewalk'. The parallels between Cornuché's vision of food and femininity and aviation's use of the pretty young stewardess are obvious.

By the time Juan and Betty Trippe patronized Maxim's it was already a huge success, popular with the rich and famous of the 1930s such as Edward VIII, Marcel Proust, Greta Garbo and Marlène Dietrich.[15] As outlined below, when Juan and Betty Trippe honeymooned in 1928 aboard the German steamship the SS *Bremen* they dined in a version of the Ritz restaurant located on the ship's upper deck. When the famous upper lounge of the Boeing 747 is considered, it is easy to see where Trippe may have gotten his early inspiration for recreating fine restaurant dining in transit. During the belle époque, Maxim's was at the forefront of a new gastronomy, boasting a dining experience incorporating mixed soups, eight to ten entrées, roasts, salads and desserts. The restaurant was typical of how Parisian restaurants emerged from the nineteenth and into the twentieth century as objects of reverie: they were brands of daydream and desire, referenced frequently in written and spoken word. In short, Parisian restaurant culture represented the height of personal gastronomic pleasure in the modern world; in the words of one historian, it 'kept modernity's bounty from overwhelming the individual; every customer believed he could have anything he desired but he needed only confront his own small portion'.[16] In its vision of abundance, it resembled the 'American Plan' meal which was a feature of American hotels in the nineteenth century, but there the similarities end. Whereas a guest at an American Plan meal could gluttonously wolf down as much food as desired for a flat cost, French fine dining was distinguished

---

[15] History of Maxim's, http://maxims-de-paris.com/en/restaurant (accessed 16 January 2018).
[16] Rebecca Spang, *The Invention of the Restaurant: Paris and Modern Gastronomic Pleasure* (Harvard: Harvard University Press, 2000), 239.

by high price, smaller portions and the slow, careful ritual of ordering, eating and conversing.[17] It was this multi-course cuisine delivered from rolling carts that seduced Juan Trippe, and which the company was later to duplicate in the Boeing 707. Following their first visit in 1936, the Trippes visited Maxim's again in 1952, striking the deal which would see Maxim's provide Pan Am flights with food for the next twenty years. Betty Trippe, who – as her diary entries prove – was never very easy to please, recorded approvingly that 'lunch at Maxim's was delicious. The woodcock sautéed in wine and the Camembert cheese were a real treat'.[18] It was a rare seal of approval from the first lady of the American airline industry.

Having airline food prepared by culinary professionals was, in itself, nothing new. In the 1920s American airline Transcontinental Air Transport (or TAT, which was later to become Howard Hughes's TWA) boasted that its food was prepared by the Fred Harvey Company, a chain of restaurants that provided meals at railroad stations. This system harked back to American transport in the nineteenth century, where travel by steamboat was linked to the railways. The Fred Harvey chain's numerous locations across the American rail network provided a rough blueprint for providing food en masse to travellers via airport-based flight kitchens, yet the company never prepared special meals for in-flight service nor opened locations in airports, sticking instead to train stations. What's more, its cheap snacky fare was resolutely American and uncomplicated, chiefly consisting of lemonade and cookies. In the 1930s rival airline Boeing Air Transport went one better by serving food prepared by Chicago's renowned Palmer House Hotel, but the food was similarly straightforwardly American – chicken, fruit and rolls – and served on paper plates. Eastern and American Airlines followed suit, linking with the Marriott hotel corporation, which now began to situate its catering operations in airports.

In 1936 United Airlines broke the mould by hiring professional chef Don Magarell to transform its menus. Magarell introduced a greater variety of dishes, whose names were printed in both English and French, and convinced the company to locate its kitchens at major airports. And yet, at the same time as American carriers were starting to embrace European gastronomic influences, the Second World War intervened, disrupting civilian transport by prioritizing war cargoes. Post-war, the trend of locating flight kitchens staffed

---

[17] See A. K. Sandoval-Strauss, *Hotel: An American History* (New Haven, CT: Yale University Press, 2007); Jefferson Williamson, *The American Hotel: An Anecdotal History* (New York: Knopf, 1930), 202.
[18] Trippe, *The Diary and Letters*, 188.

by professional caterers at airports continued, evidenced through the expansion of the Sky Chefs franchise, an American nationwide catering chain. The move towards professionalism now gathered pace, with the signature of a chef differentiating an airline and promising a bonanza in the industry. International airlines began working more closely with chefs, for example, the Italian airline Alitalia commenced service in 1947 with dinners prepared by chefs of the Rosati restaurant of Rome's Via Veneto.[19] Meanwhile, Brazilian airline VARIG ramped up the Old World charm by announcing that its Rio de Janeiro to New York flight would feature food prepared by a chef who had once cooked for the last Russian royal family, the Romanovs.[20] More notable still, Air France's luxury services were becoming increasingly popular with international customers, with its 'Parisien spécial' to New York offering private cabins, welcome champagne and dishes created by professional chefs including Marcel Chémery from Paris restaurant Chez Ledoyen and Gaston Chatelet, head chef of the cruise liner *Lafayette*, as well as Fernand Deveaux, pastry chef of the luxury liner *Normandie*.[21] The movement of top international chefs away from the ocean liners and towards the airlines illustrated the growing glamour of flying. The short-lived *Normandie* (1932–46), for example, was widely regarded as the most lavish ship ever to sail: the first-class grand salon was 282 feet long and three decks high, decorated with onyx, crystal, gold and glass fountains carved by art deco designer René Lalique, and entered via a spectacular staircase and twenty-foot-high bronze doors.[22]

These trends demanded a big response from America's international airline and explain why, in embracing Maxim's, the company decided to link with a specific restaurant brand, and a French one at that. Although Pan Am had pioneered the frozen airline meal, everyone knew that the industrial quality of the food produced by inventor William Maxson's company was poor. Perhaps indicative of a fundamental biological survival mechanism, food that looks unattractive tends to be unappetizing. An internal company memorandum from 1948 (just after William Maxson's death) echoed that composed by executive Melville Stone in late 1946, complaining 'the Maxson food system is not satisfactory and should be abandoned. The food does not look good and the only foods that do not taste queer are the potatoes and cooked apples'.[23] Another internal report admitted

---

[19] Foss, *Food in the Air and Space*, 27.
[20] www.varig-airlines.com/en/50.htm. Thanks to Inez Amaral de Sampaio.
[21] Desgrandchamps and Donzel, *Cuisine à bord*, 11.
[22] Sarah Edington, *The Captain's Table: Life and Dining on the Great Ocean Liners* (London: National Maritime Museum, 2005), 19.
[23] D. S. Ingalls to Trippe, 12 March 1948. 'Johannesburg Flight', First & Inaugural Flights Box 2, Flight & Route Information Series, folder 29-10. University of Miami digital collections, Pan Am material. Courtesy of Gabrielle Williams.

that the Maxson disposable plate – consisting of pressed cardboard and plastic covering – tainted the food to the extent that the various entrées and vegetables were often indistinguishable in taste and appearance.[24] Pan Am had to aspire to better things than homogeneous mush. There was a problem, however. In its rush to embrace the new technology of oven-heating pre-prepared frozen meals, the company had remodelled the galleys in its airplanes. Any reversion to non-frozen food not only opened up the possibility of non-standardized fare – which was deemed unsafe – but would mean huge costs in galley redesign. In short, the oven-heated frozen airline meal was going to stay, but the quality of the product needed huge improvement. For this reason, Melville Stone, who had first urged Trippe to sever the company's reliance on food from Maxson's oven company and instead pursue culinary excellence, was in favour of a partnership with New York's exclusive Waldorf Astoria hotel.[25] Instead, Trippe mulled over his options before plumping for Maxim's and sealing the American–French partnership.

The choice of Maxim's spoke to the internationalizing ambitions of the company in the Cold War era. Although the kitchens preparing these meals were located on Rue Rodier, in a separate district of Paris from the original bistro, the restaurant's chefs prepared them. While other airlines came to embrace sole master chefs (like Raymond Oliver of the Michelin three-star restaurant Le Grand Vefour who was recruited by French airline UTA in the 1970s) Pan Am's signature First Class President Special menu of the 1960s was a collaborative effort devised by the best chefs from Maxim's.[26] Maxim's supplied the food to the company's catering divisions, which were located in various international locations.[27] Most food was prepared fresh in flight kitchens located at the major airports. Some entrées even came direct from Paris, after being prepared at Maxim's, flash-frozen and transported to the United States.[28] Menus were changed every three months for both first-class and economy service,[29] and the food itself was subject to techniques to ensure maximum freshness. For instance, the lobsters that arrived from Newfoundland to in-flight services headquarters were alive, packaged in thick clumps of seaweed. After arrival, they were transformed into

---

[24] C. C. Snowden memo, 'Frozen food versus conventional food', 23 March 1948. 'Johannesburg Flight', First & Inaugural Flights Box 2, Flight & Route Information Series, folder 29-10. University of Miami digital collections, Pan Am material. Courtesy of Gabrielle Williams.

[25] Melville Stone memorandum, 5 December 1946, University of Miami digital collections, Pan Am material. Courtesy of Gabrielle Williams.

[26] Foss, *Food in the Air and Space*, 75.

[27] Interview with Barrie Fewster, 23 January 2018.

[28] Interview with Dian Groh, 12 January 2018.

[29] Interview with Cornelis Van Aalst, 5 February 2018.

Lobster Thermidor by Maxim's Chef de Cuisine Roger Grosjean before being flash-frozen and stored in enormous deep-freeze facilities.[30]

In 1956, and four years into the landmark partnership, airline food's place in the world of haute cuisine was secured when Pan Am and Maxim's won three prizes at the International Gastronomic Exhibition in Frankfurt, West Germany. Closely linked to the rise of global capitalism, international exhibitions first appeared in the nineteenth century, indeed Maxim's itself was closely linked to the Parisian event of 1900. In the Cold War context of the mid-twentieth century, exhibitions like that in Frankfurt became an important means of international communication and the showcasing of cultural capital in which the display of food was central.[31] Known popularly as the Culinary Olympics, the Frankfurt Gastronomic Exhibition (*Internationale Kochkunst Ausstellung*) was first established in 1900 and at the time was the largest and most prestigious culinary exhibition in the world. The Pan Am–Maxim's exhibition was designed to resemble a tranquil Parisian restaurant juxtaposed above by a large model of a Clipper airplane illuminated by spotlights. Remarkably, though, the actual food on display was frozen. Dishes prepared by Maxim's chef Louis Barth were arranged in a freezer display case surrounded by flowers, champagnes, wines, cognacs and 'President Special' menus (Figure 3.2). Maxim's owner, Louis Vaudable, was on hand to collect the gold medal, special citation and prize of honour on behalf of the airline and the restaurant.[32]

The landmark award of a gold medal for *frozen food* signalled gastronomy's surprising embrace of airline food. It illustrated the revolutionary success of a partnership just four years old. In 1952, on behalf of the company, Thomas Nolan (who joined Pan Am in 1943 and was later Pan Am catering manager at Heathrow and Paris) signed the original contract with Louis Vaudable of the famous French restaurant. His son Ed recalls his father's long business luncheons at Maxim's, where menus were discussed at length, followed by trips to Maxim's wine cellar, where the most suitable wines were selected.[33] Thereafter, groups of Pan Am managers (accompanied by their wives) regularly visited the Parisian restaurant to witness its chefs at work and were regularly enthralled by

---

[30] Lou Berman, 'Pan Am's Haute Cuisine: Praised to the High Heavens', *Clipper* (March 2012), 7.
[31] See Nelleke Teughels, 'Introduction', in Peter Scholliers and Nelleke Teughels (eds), *A Taste of Progress: Food at International and World Exhibitions in the Nineteenth and Twentieth Centuries* (Farnham: Ashgate, 2015), 1–10.
[32] *Pan Am System Sales Clipper*, vol. 14, no. 12, December 1956. University of Miami Libraries digital collections, Pan Am material (uncatalogued).
[33] Interview with Ed Nolan, 21 February 2018.

Figure 3.2 The aluminium container airline meal as haute cuisine, Maxim's, Paris, 1950s. Courtesy: Ed Nolan.

its splendour. Such trips culminated in an excursion outside Paris, usually to the Bordeaux region to sample wines.[34] The Parisian glamour attached to the partnership demonstrates the limitations of a reductively scientific approach to airline eating. Naturally, altitude, humidity and cabin pressure affect the flavour and taste of food. But although foods contain flavour molecules, the flavour of those molecules is also created in the brain. Flavour lies largely in the mind, as sensory neuroscientists have proven.[35] Thus many a wine consumed mid-air may have technically tasted worse than on the ground, but the ambience and glamour attached to the idea that the wine had been specially selected by Maxim's – its famous jaunty golden scrawl emblazoning Pan Am's menus – ensured enjoyment regardless for many.

Close collaboration with such a renowned restaurant as Maxim's meant that, naturally, certain dishes were a little too avant-garde for some passengers' tastes. One employee recalled 'we had on the menu Jugged Hare for a short time; that

---

[34] Lloyd Wilson to Louis Vaudable, 26 August 1959. Ed Nolan private collection.
[35] See Bob Holmes, *Flavor: The Science of Our Most Neglected* Sense (New York: W. W. Norton, 2017).

was definitely a Maxim's special, crew had a terrible time pushing that dish! Not a normal American favorite!'[36] In 1970 Pan Am's management asked Maxim's to cut prices, which the restaurant refused to do, claiming that the quality of the products would have decreased and, in 1971, following Trippe's retirement, the partnership dissolved.[37] However, the features of fine dining inspired by Maxim's lingered long. Right up until the airline's demise, customers in First and Clipper class would have their coats removed and hung by staff in a reserved closet while they settled down into leather and sheepskin seats to enjoy their refreshing glass of champagne.[38]

Whether popular culture 'trickles down' from above or forms organically 'from below' is a matter of dispute. In terms of the American public's embrace of French cuisine, however, Pan Am's relationship with Maxim's, coupled – significantly – with the introduction of economy class flights, predated Julia Child's *The French Chef* by ten years. In the 1950s the company sought to democratize the enjoyment of European cuisine, with one advert promising 'a man with no training as a gourmet can eat his way half way across the Atlantic between cocktails and coffee'. Explaining that passengers could spend over half of the seven-hour trip between New York and the Eiffel Tower doing nothing but consuming the 'elegance of Maxim's of Paris', the gastronomic experience of the passenger was imagined thus:

> An hour out of Boston, off the coast of Nova Scotia, the passenger is having his consommé or sampling a shrimp cocktail. He has already studied the wine list and selected a vintage to accompany his entrée. He might prefer a red Bordeaux with his filet mignon or Pouilly Fuisse with his lobster thermidor … The plane is off the coast of Newfoundland at 8pm. The passenger, having had cocktails, canapes and appetizer, is enjoying his main course, a stately procession of meals designed to be enjoyed at a leisurely pace … After cheese and salad, when the plane is far to the south of Greenland, pastry and fruit are on the menu and the traveller can round off his meal with flaming crepes suzette, flipped paper thin with Cordon Bleu dexterity.

This vision of a lengthy, slow dinner spoke to the French ideal and countered the American reputation for fast, loud and vulgar overeating. Demonstrating that the journey was just as much a culinary adventure as the actual destination, after

---

[36] Email correspondence with Lesley van der Schroeff, 15 January 2018.
[37] Dian Stirn Groh with Becky Snider Sprecher, 'Parisian Partnership'.
[38] Pan Am advertisement, *Airline World*, 17 October 1986. University of Miami special collections, Pan Am collection no. 341, series I, box 61, folder 7.

arrival the passenger did not even have to bother setting foot in an authentic Parisian restaurant for dinner:

> Since it's breakfast hours in Paris, the passenger may prefer to forego the snack and have his croissant and café au lait in the shadow of the Eiffel Tower. The traveller, of course, gains six hours by flying back from Paris to New York. He could, for example, leave Paris at 5pm, have dinner on the jet and arrive in Manhattan in time for the theatre and a good night's sleep.[39]

The Old and the New Worlds

Pan Am's pre-war relationship with the art deco movement was a harbinger of the latter fusion of the Old and the New. Art deco's style was both primitive and modernist, combining motifs such as the Aztec sunburst with the aerodynamism of aluminium and reinserting the aesthetics of skilled local handicraft into mass production.[40] This theme was to return in the post-war period when, although the service remained elite, the number of Americans willing and able to experience a slice of the Old World was expanding. Setting out to educate the palettes of their customers in European – and particularly French – culinary culture was part of the company's contribution to the American post-war ideal of 'glamour'. If the Pan Am flight attendant embodied that very notion, the emergence of the concept itself in popular culture is significant. Some historians point to the food and drink service provided by the Parisian barmaid of the belle époque, and immortalized by artists of the period, as signifying the birth of 'glamour' as part of consumer culture, while others look to Hollywood's golden age.[41] Through its food relationship with Maxim's, Pan Am embraced both. The partnership encapsulated Pan Am's embrace of both the Old World, where antiquity was highly esteemed ('our blood runs blue' was a company slogan), and the New World, where newness itself was a virtue. Thus, the aristocratically named chateaubriand (named after the noble French writer of the Victorian period François-René de Chateaubriand) was heated in the most modern American-manufactured ovens and fussy old Parisian dining rituals would be mimicked

---

[39] 'How to eat your way to Europe in jet luxury', *Sales Clipper*, vol. 16, no. 9, September 1958, p. 3, University of Miami digital collections, Pan Am material.

[40] See Richard Pellis, *Modernist America: Art, Music, Movies, and the Globalization of American Culture* (New Haven, CT: Yale University Press, 2012).

[41] Kathleen Barry, *Femininity in Flight: A History of Flight Attendants* (Durham, NC: Duke University Press, 2007), 4.

within a technologically cutting-edge environment. 'We are not trying to be "the world's most experienced anachronism": a 21st century airline with the graciousness of an 18th century restaurant,' insisted Pan Am's head of food and beverages in the late 1960s, explaining instead that the company's 'integrated system' sought to combine frozen food with locally produced items, blending the Old with the New.[42]

In line with these high dining ideals, the signature service – the President Special – was duly flooded with Gallic content. The 1950s witnessed the introduction of a flight itself dubbed the President Special (after the menu) an elite Stratocruiser service offered to just 75 passengers, all First Class, on a small and exclusive once-weekly New York–London overnight flight, which returned to New York in the same day and was staffed by just one steward and one stewardess. The inaugural menu of this new VIP service was footed with a quote from the great French gastronome Auguste Escoffier: '*La bonne cuisine* est la base du véritable bonheur' ('Good food is the foundation of genuine happiness'). The eight courses started with a choice of *hors d'oeuvre* (ham, game, salmon or caviar), followed by *potage* (turtle soup or paprika sticks), *entrées* (roast rib eye of beef or Cornish game hen), *legumes* (buttered peas or potato croquettes), *salade* (hearts of lettuce), *fromages* (cheese selection), *dessert* (a selection of pastries) and *fruits* (fruit basket). The food was accompanied by a selection of coffees, white and red wine (Bourgogne Blanc and Bordeaux Rouge), champagne (Brut Millésimé) and liqueurs (chiefly Cognac).[43] Arguably, only the glassware accompanying the President Special was unequivocally 'American' – featuring the US imperial eagle, for flight attendants mindful of proper measures, the tip of the eagle's wings represented the top filling point, memorized by staff through the saying 'don't drown the eagle'.[44] In blurring the culinary boundaries between the Old World and the New, the President Special symbolized an elite and inherently transnational cuisine.

With the arrival of the jet age and the Boeing 707 in 1958 came the refinement of the original President Special to include cart service. Cart service directly mimicked service in Maxim's but was also the latest example of the function of food-as-entertainment, as embodied by the early pursers. Pan Am introduced cart service with the intention that the replication of Parisian high dining rituals would serve as a form of in-flight entertainment complete with ornate silver

[42] *Wing Tips*, vol. 1, no. 10, November 1967, University of Miami digital collections, Pan Am material.
[43] Email correspondence with Rebecca Sprecher, 25 January 2018.
[44] Interview with Sybille Holder, 15 March 2018.

presentation bowls. It bears repeating that food and drink was a greater part of in-flight entertainment than today's norm of passengers availing of a number of audiovisual distractions. In first class, meat was served from a carving board usually featuring chateaubriand, rack of lamb or pork. One former flight attendant recalled her anxiety one Thanksgiving when, for the first time in her life, she was required to carve a turkey, fearing that the bird would go flying off the cart into someone's lap. Thankfully, without her even raising the carving knife, a male passenger announced to everyone that this was his first Thanksgiving away from home and asked if he could have the honour of doing the job. In an appropriate blending of the American and the French, he was rewarded with a bottle of Dom Pérignon champagne when he left the aircraft.[45]

The mid-air carving of the Thanksgiving turkey may have been a homespun Americanism worthy of artist Norman Rockwell's famous all-smiles painting of a family meal *Freedom from Want* (1943), but Pan Am's post-war culinary direction pointed definitely towards Europe. In 1955 Rockwell himself was recruited by the company to fly around the world and create a sketch book of alluring foreign foods, places and people. Pan Am's new-found embrace of European gastronomy was based upon the notion of proper education and supervision of food. Catering Superintendent Louis Berman, who served with Pan Am for four decades from the 1950s to the 1980s, recalled that the real genius behind something so ostensibly American as the 'President Special' service was Kurt Knuessi, like him a graduate of a prestigious Swiss cookery school, the Ecole Hotelière de la Société des Hoteliers of Lausanne, Switzerland. Knuessi reported to another graduate of a prestigious school of service, Phil Parrot, who had trained at Cornell University's School of Hotel Management in Ithaca, New York. In turn, meal evaluation sessions took place under the critical eye of the company's vice president, Herb Milley.[46] Similarly, Pan Am's first-class food options also provided an opportunity for parents to educate their offspring in good food. One former flight attendant remembers a father attempting to get his two small sons to try caviar, only to be met with a simultaneous and deafening 'yuck' when they took one look at the food in front of them.[47] In 1961, in an effort to amend its fare to meet the needs of child passengers, the company reverted to the classics of American cuisine it had offered in the early days: hot dogs and hamburgers. Children now had a choice between the regular Clipper

---

[45] Email correspondence with Barbara Sharfstein, 15 January 2018.
[46] Lou Berman, 'Pan Am's Haute Cuisine: Praised to the High Heavens', *Clipper* (March 2012), 7.
[47] Email correspondence with Barbara Sharfstein, 15 January 2018.

menu (featuring dishes not commonly associated with the child's palette such as Lobster Thermidor and Pheasant L'Armagnac) and a special children's menu featuring burgers, hot dogs, French fries, ice cream and milk.[48]

VIP Diners

Consistent with the notion of catering for children, the glamour of dining Pan Am inevitably led to unreasonable behaviour from some passengers. A common refrain among employees was 'God has lots of funny children and they *all* fly Pan Am.'[49] For example, one former flight attendant recalled a first-class passenger who had neglected to book a seat for the dining service in the upper lounge of the 747 and who, when refused service, behaved like a spoiled child, throwing his napkin away and sitting on the floor, arms and legs crossed, before stubbornly declaring 'then I don't want to eat at all!'[50] Perhaps the passenger's reaction is better understood by the fact that few other experiences symbolized the twin notions of twentieth-century American abundance and affluence like Pan Am's first-class food service aboard the 747.

Although dependent on route and time of flight, standard first-class food service aboard a 747 was as follows: a welcome drink of champagne and/or orange juice would be served prior to take-off. After take-off drink orders would be taken, with cocktails made to order on board and served with a ramekin of mixed warmed nuts. After cocktails were finished, the meal service would start. If requested, tray tables were connected with an insert to create a table for two. A flower in a vase was placed in front of each passenger as well as individual salt and pepper shakers, and a roll-up napkin was provided with the silverware. A cart would appear with hors d'oeuvres such as caviar, chopped egg and chilled vodka, as well as other delicacies. Then it would be time for soup or salad, followed by the main course. All main courses were plated in the galley with the exception of the roast beef cart from which meat was theatrically sliced, accompanied by mixed vegetables, potatoes, jus, mustard or horseradish. After the main course, cheeses were presented, accompanied by fruit, bread, butter and crackers. Throughout the meal service wine was offered, usually two reds and a white. After cheeses came the dessert card: ice cream with various sauces,

[48] *International Herald Tribune*, 19 February 1961.
[49] Interview with Winnifred Omodt, 26 February 2018.
[50] Interview with Cornelis Van Aalst, 5 February 2018.

whipped cream and chopped nuts. Following dessert, coffee or tea was offered with a selection of liqueurs.[51] The decoration of food with parsley provided a signature Pan Am flourish. Passengers were also given the choice of service at their seat or the use of the large galley for self-service, and snacks and drinks were provided throughout the journey. On flights that departed too late for breakfast and too early for lunch a 'Special Brunch' was served; commencing with a Bloody Mary and ending with champagne or coffee, the special brunch could comprise grapefruit, filet of sole, omelette, lamp chop or fruit, according to taste.[52] First-class passengers could dine in the upper lounge of the 747 only after making a reservation (like in a restaurant) and would be seated at four-person tables decorated with flowers. It was the responsibility of the staff member occupying the newly titled role of 'flight director' to pass through the plane and discreetly judge which passengers might make suitable dining companions. Since many passengers in first class travelled alone, choosing four individuals to dine together demanded a judicious selection process. Often, too, staff would adopt a peace-brokering spirit reminiscent of the United Nations, placing people of ostensibly opposing backgrounds – for example, Arabs and Israelis – on the same table, and thus pre-empting dialogue over dinner.[53]

The 'United Nations' arrangement of upper lounge seating spoke directly to the pan American ideal, yet the quality and renown of food aboard Pan Am flights ensured that it had become the chosen airline of the rich and famous before the 747 and its upper bulge. To fly Pan Am promised indulgence and, at times, an escapist over-indulgence. Film star Maureen O'Hara recalled how the abundance offered by Pan Am afforded her the chance to break away from the constant round of diets demanded of a female movie star and she would look forward to gluttonously devouring the 'always delicious' food.[54] Fellow actress Lana Turner liked Pan Am's first-class food so much she always requested a doggie bag so that she could take her leftovers away with her.[55] A special menu was often prepared for VIPs such as heads of state. Presidential aides (or equivalent) would present the relevant Pan Am commissary manager with a special menu, after which it was up to the commissary team to ensure it was realized in the air, complete with unique commemorative menu card. This

[51] Interview with Cornelis Van Aalst, 5 February 2018.
[52] 'Preparation of Gourmet Food' (undated), University of Miami special collections, Pan Am collection no. 341, series I, box 292, folder 5.
[53] Interview with Sybille Holder, 15 March 2018.
[54] Maureen O'Hara interview on 'Come fly with me – The story of Pan Am' (BBC Documentary broadcast 28 January 2012, BBC Four).
[55] Email correspondence with Barbara Sharfstein, 15 January 2018.

process, reserved for the most prestigious of passengers, ensured that dignitaries did not experience any surprises or disappointments, with favourite dishes becoming well known. President Lyndon B. Johnson, for example, was said to be never happier than when he was mid-air dining on Cornish hen, a type of bird developed from cross-breeding and achieving great popularity in the 1950s and 1960s.[56] On occasion, VIPs instructed that the company surprise the relevant dignitary with its own special menu; for example, one commissioned for the flight of Japan's Prince Akihito from San Francisco to Tokyo, in October 1953, was geared towards the Hawaiian layover – offering a smattering of Japanese options such as sushi and sake but dominated by Hawaiian foods such as fried shrimp, kokies, sandwiches, pickles and peanuts. Most often, though, VIP menus catered to individual taste to the extent of replicating favourite dishes from the individual's home cuisine. Facilitating the favourite food of some VIPs could prove challenging. When Sukarno, the first president of Indonesia (in office 1945–67), flew Pan Am, strict religious requirements were observed in keeping with his Muslim faith. Sukarno was extremely fond of durian fruit and no flight chartered by him would be allowed to depart without a generous supply of it. There was one problem, recalled Pan Am staff: durian fruit smelt 'to high heavens'.[57] The aroma of durian, a big fruit with a hard shell and sharp thorns native to Southeast Asia, has been compared by one food writer to 'a mix between turpentine and onions, garnished with a gym sock'[58] and merely trying to suppress the smell was a challenge for flight staff.

A 1997 survey of upscale executives conducted by *Executive Travel* magazine revealed that, for first-class passengers, the most common bugbear about airplane food service was not the quality of the fare itself but not being able to take one's choice from the menu.[59] One retired flight attendant recalled how, for one passenger whom she encountered in her second year as a Pan Am flight attendant in 1971, this proved a particularly sore point. She was preparing for take-off from JFK to London by collecting entrée orders from the sixty or so passengers in first class. Passenger after passenger requested the plane's limited supply of prime rib, a firm Pan Am favourite, except for one business traveller, who didn't even look up when she asked what he wanted. When she stopped

[56] *Pan American Clipper*, vol. 25, no. 2, 1 November 1966.
[57] Interview with Louis Berman, 24 January 2018.
[58] Joseph Stromberg, 'Why does the durian fruit smell so terrible?', Smithsonian.com, 30 November 2012 (accessed 24 January 2018).
[59] Geoff Tansey, 'Food for thought: Your verdict on airline catering', *Executive Travel*, September 1997, 10.

by again, after everyone else had ordered, the man finally looked up. Now he wanted the prime rib, too.

'I'm sorry sir, it's all been ordered' she informed him.

'Do you know who I am?' he demanded. 'I could buy up every seat here.'

'But you didn't, sir' she replied 'and now I'm sorry, but it's all gone.'

As a last-gasp effort to get the prime rib, he then told her to tell 'some other passenger' in the cabin that she had miscounted the orders and give him that prime rib instead. She refused. 'I only learned who the passenger was two weeks after the encounter when I was summoned by my bosses to respond to a very angry complaint letter claiming I hadn't treated him "like a first class passenger" and demanding that I be sacked.' Thankfully, she recalls, 'our supervisors never assumed that passenger complaints were well-founded'. And, in this case, after hearing my side, the managers actually said, 'thank you for doing the right thing'.[60] The passenger, as it turns out, was 45th US President Donald Trump, then aged twenty-five.

Another former flight attendant recalled that her worst celebrity experience around food was with an inebriated former Beatle, Paul McCartney, and his wife Linda, who were travelling with their infant daughter Stella aboard a 747. After food service it was requested that she take Stella to the bathroom, where she had to assist the girl in her toilet 'including wiping' – a duty certainly not expected of flight attendants but illustrative of the fact that some viewed them as mid-air mothers, a gendered expectation around food service which is discussed later.[61] Although management could side with the food server, Pan Am's elite status and attention to detail ensured that finicky complaints were dealt with seriously. In 1988, a complaint from a first-class passenger over the incorrect use of tongs led to a company missive instructing that the 'spoon and fork' technique (of cupping delicate food items between both items of cutlery) must *always* take place with the fork on top and the spoon on bottom.[62] On the other hand, many retired flight attendants recall very pleasant conversations with the rich and famous over food. During one food service the actor Sidney Poitier, one recalls, asked her why she looked so glum. She explained that she had had an argument with her boyfriend, who happened to be the purser aboard the flight. Poitier stopped eating, placed his plate to one side and rose from his seat, calling over the purser and performing some impromptu relationship counselling to them both.[63] Many

[60] Interview with Winnifred Omodt, 26 February 2018.
[61] Interview with Margie Thompson, 15 March 2018.
[62] Pan Am Monthly operational bulletin, vol. 18, no. 5, June 1988, University of Miami digital collections, Pan Am material.
[63] Interview with Donna Valdes, 15 March 2018.

also aver that the worst behaved and most entitled passengers were not in fact celebrities or VIPs but travel agents.

Alcohol

For many Pan Am passengers the notion of an elite airline was intertwined with an over-indulgence they imagined typical of the high life and, for many, this was synonymous with alcoholic inebriation. During prohibition, thirsty Americans hankering for an alcoholic drink could fly with Pan Am to Havana, Cuba. Mail transport was then the company's stock-in-trade, but when loads were light Pan Am's agents would stand outside the company offices on Biscayne Boulevard in Miami promising 'you can bathe in Bacardi two hours from now!'[64] It is alleged that one such passenger was the infamous gangster Al Capone, who is reputed to have flown Pan Am to Havana with five other men, enjoying Cuban rum before returning on a flight laden with liquor which was later intercepted by US Customs.[65] Although alcohol was illicit in this period, its availability at a destination not far from American shores added a touch of adventure to the early reputation of flying. Betty Trippe – who recalled, with inimitable disgust, being propositioned over dinner by Capone and his 'thugs in their flashy tropical suits' at a hotel in Nassau, Bahamas, in 1929 – relayed the story of one passenger getting carried away on one of the early Miami to Havana flights. 'A man boarded the plane with a bottle of whiskey in his pocket', she wrote, but halfway to Key West became 'very drunk and tried to get into the cockpit'. He was prevented from doing so by 'a very dignified conservative type, the Treasurer of Pan Am'. As the two men wrestled wildly across the aisle, the treasurer's trousers were ripped off. When they finally landed 'an American flag had to be brought out, so the treasurer, having retrieved his pince-nez, could disembark with some dignity and modesty'.[66]

Having experienced the glamour of dining on sea liners, Juan Trippe was keen to recreate the experience in the air to give Pan Am a competitive edge. While prohibition, which included the service of alcohol in-flight, initially stymied these efforts, the repeal of the legislation in 1933 created

---

[64] Don Wright, 'First Flight', University of Miami special collections, Pan Am collection no. 341, series I, box 28, folder 2.

[65] Interview with George Kuhn, July 1958, University of Miami special collections, Pan Am collection no. 341, series I, box 15, folder 13.

[66] Trippe, *The Diary and Letters*, 12.

new opportunities for dining accompanied by alcohol. Aviation journalist
Carl B. Allen, aboard a Pan Am flight to Cuba shortly after prohibition ended,
wrote of the restorative powers of a glass of beer to the weary traveller, the
tipple providing 'a pleasant tingle through my blood, lulling nameless aches in
my back and chest and a shortness of breath resulting from a persistent cold,
long exhausting hours and too little sleep'; as the descent to Havana started he
saw 'high on the hill-top in the centre of the city a sign to hearten travellers
by air … the single word "Bacardi" in giant letters'.[67] The increased size of the
Boeing 314 Clipper (1938) saw the introduction of an amply stocked bar.[68] In
the same decade, and as detailed previously, Pan Am's development of bases
on the Pacific atolls necessitated food and drink provisioning from ships. One
lead member of the company's 'Pacific expedition' (as it was known) recalled
that the ship's steward, a relative of a Pan Am pilot and a recovering alcoholic,
was sent on the expedition in the hope that he would stay off the bottle. In
charge of all provisioning, the steward reverted to old habits and was 'always
drunk', except no one could figure out where he was getting the alcohol from.
The truth was revealed when the steward drunkenly threw a wine bottle out
of a porthole one evening, hitting a fellow Pan Am employee on the head. The
ship's supplies were duly searched and it was revealed that, unbeknown to the
ship's crew, the company had sent over several cases of wine which the steward,
travelling below decks to 'check temperatures' on the food supplies, had been
steadily consuming.[69]

With the advent of transatlantic flight, the blurring of the Old and New
Worlds would also bring inspiration and interchange when it came to alcoholic
beverages and the era of the flying boats led to the invention of new drinks,
such as the famous Irish Coffee, which originated from the flying boat station
in Foynes in the west of Ireland. In 1943, following its departure for New York,
a Pan Am flying boat encountered bad weather conditions and radioed back to
Foynes to inform them of the plane's return. The staff of the Foynes restaurant
were called back to work and chef Joe Sheridan, when tasked with preparing
something to give a lift to the weary passengers, decided to add some Irish
whiskey to their coffee. One passenger thanked the chef afterwards for the

---

[67] Carl B. Allen, undated and untitled note on Clipper flight to Havana, Carl B. Allen papers, box 8,
     folder 7, WVRAC.
[68] Stirn Groh and Snider Sprecher, 'Dining Aloft', 121–4.
[69] Interview with George Kuhn, July 1958, University of Miami special collections, Pan Am collection
     no. 341, series I, box 15, folder 13.

delicious coffee, asking if it was Brazilian, to which Sheridan replied 'no, it was Irish'.[70]

In 1946 the International Air Transport Association resolved 'that alcoholic beverages will not in any case be provided free of charge'.[71] Passenger demand meant that this resolution was soon to change, and by the late 1940s Pan Am was offering free alcohol on transatlantic flights. It still charged for drinks on Pacific routes, however, a policy which caused some confusion even – it seems – among the company's top brass. After being unexpectedly charged $1.50 for a cocktail on a Pacific flight, Juan Trippe himself is reputed to have changed the policy immediately after landing, making alcohol free on all routes.[72] The free alcohol policy extended to Latin American services, ushering in the now-standard mini bottle of wine, which first appeared in the late 1940s. As Carl B. Allen observed, the Second World War 'literally handed South American trade to us' and Pan Am, 'in true Yankee fashion', snatched it for the United States.[73] As they did so, however, they had to adapt to Latin American cultures. The company explained to its Hispanic customers that 'the North American habit of drinking water with a meal, to a Latin American, seems insipid'; Pan Am's 'culinary experts' had therefore collaborated with a 'well known company' to devise a mini-bottle of wine ('botellita de vino') to be served with food; this innovation also saved time – passengers could choose simply between a mini-bottle of sherry or Chablis, which eliminated the need to consult the extensive wine list. At the time, this was such a novelty that passengers were urged to take the empty mini-bottle home with them as a souvenir of their journey.[74]

Wine aside, there remained a key difference between service in the air and one of the norms of restaurant dining: tipping. The gratitude of passengers for good service is illustrated by an account from a staff publication, which told how an employee recently promoted to purser had taken a silver plate of change gathered from cocktail service into the bathroom in order to count it in peace (on certain flights, passengers were still charged for cocktails, unlike 'straight' alcoholic drinks). Interrupted by a call button, the purser forgot all about the plate of coins until several hours later and hurried back to the toilet to count the

[70] Foynes Flying Boat and Maritime Museum, Irish Coffee, https://www.flyingboatmuseum.com/irish-coffee-center/ (accessed 12 January 2018).

[71] Report on Resolution 5 of the European Traffic Conference of IATA, 27 May 1946. Truman Library, George C. Neal papers, box 18-I.

[72] Foss, *Food in the Air and Space*, 71.

[73] Carl B. Allen, undated and untitled article on Latin America, Carl B. Allen papers, box 1, folder 5, WVRAC.

[74] *Caminos del aire*, Volumen XI, Núm. 7, October and November 1948, University of Miami digital collections, Pan Am material.

plate for missing money; instead she found that it contained thirty dollars more than when she had left it.[75] Yet despite the value added to service by individual flight attendants, the company always discouraged the custom. According to one account, this was because Trippe himself was a niggardly tipper and disliked the custom,[76] but the company insisted that the policy derived from the need to ensure efficient service was unencumbered by the handling of money. This seems dubious because, as mentioned, up until the 1950s Pan Am charged for all alcoholic drinks, involving a good deal of awkward handling of cash as passengers disposed of exotic foreign coins they no longer wanted. Before drinks became free, the company was also unresponsive to pleas from staff that drinks prices be rounded up to ensure ease of transaction, preferring to price drinks at $1.25 or $1.75 rather than a straight dollar. This frequently resulted in extended conversation and fumbling around in pockets and purses as passengers struggled to find the correct change. Given the fluctuation of exchange rates, debate and argument often broke out between servers and customers. To assist in these situations, handheld calculators were issued to staff along with a monthly list of global exchange rates. Often, flight attendants would intervene with a nickel or a dime of their own money in order to stop an endless argument and enable service to continue.[77] Alternatively, if viewed in a more benign light, Trippe's opposition to tipping can be seen as another example of how his ideal of food service at times harked back to an earlier, more egalitarian America of mass travel during which tipping was dismissed as a redundant practice, one which was – in essence – archaic and anti-republican.[78]

Trippe himself was fond of alcohol and was described in a 1949 *Time* magazine feature as a 'two-Scotches-before-dinner man'.[79] However it is likely that the 1920s incident with the drunken passenger and the American flag delayed the introduction of free alcohol on flights, something which Pan Am was slow to introduce for the stated reason that an intoxicated passenger might interfere with flight crew. By the 1950s, when alcohol had become a staple of flights, Scotch whisky was found to be the favourite tipple of the Pan Am customer and, in terms of entertainment, passengers were said to 'do more

---

[75] *Travel talk*, December 1966, University of Miami digital collections, Pan Am material.
[76] Bender and Altschul, *The Chosen Instrument*, 366.
[77] Frahm, *Above and Below the Clouds*, 142.
[78] Erby Kelly, *Public Appetite; Dining Out in Nineteenth Century Boston* (unpublished PhD dissertation, Emory University, 2010), 107.
[79] *Time*, 28 March 1949. University of Miami special collections, Pan Am collection no. 341, series I, box 62, folder 1.

drinking than reading'.[80] Predictably enough, once the almost unlimited supply of alcohol became a feature of flying, drunken passengers became a more frequent problem. One flight attendant in the Pacific/Alaska division in the 1950s wrote that drunks often 'ended up sick everywhere but in the sick bags'; on one flight she 'had a woman who threw her tray over the seat in front of her, saying she thought it was a table, and then began trying to collect trays from the other passengers'. Another 'became sick and was frantic when she lost her teeth in a sick bag'.[81] Another flight attendant recalled an overnight flight from Boston to Heathrow during which a passenger who had drunk too much brandy in the upper lounge became completely incapacitated. On departure, she had to wrap the passenger's legs around her waist while a co-worker took his arms; together they 'bumped him down the stairs', arriving in a heap at the bottom just in time for landing. The passenger had to be deplaned in a wheelchair.[82]

Although the free supply of alcohol could prove problematic, its provision as an accompaniment to food was central to the gastronomic ideal pursued by Maxim's and it is no coincidence that the partnership with the French restaurant in the 1950s ushered in its freer flow. While trips to Paris to sample French wines were occasions of great bonhomie for company executives, scientific considerations again underpinned the process. Red wines usually have to sit before being sampled; as this was not possible for in-flight service the company experts needed to choose a wine that would 'travel' well.[83] Many wines are often reported to taste more bitter when sampled in the air and fruitier, cheaper wines in fact often taste better at altitude than noble wines.[84] The company's wine experts had to take these factors into account while also considering which wines best accompanied certain dishes and commissioned wine experts to source the best wines from around the world. Their main focus was on France's Burgundy region, as well as California and South Africa, depending on the point of origin of flights. The key criteria for Pan Am's wine selectors were compatibility with food on the menu in terms of taste and national cuisine and wines that could hold their taste at altitude.[85] During the years of the Maxim's–Pan Am partnership there was, therefore, a very extensive wine list (Figure 3.3).

---

[80] 'Mile-High Kitchen' (1950), University of Miami special collections, Pan Am collection no. 341, series I, box 108, folder 3.
[81] Dunning, *Voices of My Peers*, 169.
[82] Email correspondence with Bryony Holding, 15 January 2018.
[83] Interview with Barrie Fewster, 23 January 2018.
[84] Spence, 'Tasting in the air', 13.
[85] Interview with Louis Berman, 24 January 2018.

Figure 3.3 Pan Am executives wine tasting at Maxim's, 1950s. Courtesy: Ed Nolan.

Dining out on its reputation

While it was slowly collapsing in the 1980s, the company attempted to continue dining out on its reputation for service by emphasizing alcoholic indulgence. Promotional material from the decade repeatedly mentioned the fact that 'Clipper Club' members could enjoy exclusive club service at over twenty terminals around the world, where cocktails remained on the house. A downside to in-flight drinking was incidents of drunken groping of flight attendants by male passengers, which many retired female staff recall with a roll of the eyes. Although cocktail and wine service preceded the jet age, the 1970s witnessed the freer flow of liquor to an expanded clientele. Bigger capacity meant that service became more intensive and a large part of this repetitive manual labour was based around the serving of drinks. With flight attendants now barred from serving drunken travellers by both airline policies and government regulation, safety considerations clashed with customer expectations of unceasing courtesy and ever-flowing alcohol.[86] Passengers' sense of entitlement to exclusive abundance would prove a lingering hangover from the golden age.

Although cost-cutting was an imperative in the 1980s, the airline continued to receive good reviews for its first-class food service. Renowned food critic and restaurateur George Lang, writing for leading travel magazine *Travel and Leisure*, listed Pan Am's first-class meal service between Nice and New York in its 'Best of 1986', hailing the Beluga caviar as the finest he'd ever had and gushing about the fact that the food was inspired by one of the best restaurants on the French Riviera. Such glowing endorsements were useful for the ailing airline. Lang was a big proponent of theatricality in meal service – something to which Pan Am had always aspired. The intertwining of technology and theatricality in food service was hinted at early on in the company's history through Norman Bel Geddes's elaborate lounge designs: Bel Geddes was renowned not only as an industrial designer but also as a theatre designer. Lang had theatrically snobbish appeal, to boot. According to a *New York Times* profile the Hungarian-American Lang 'invented the sort of restaurant that America's post-war nouveaux riches were hankering for' (in short, restaurants inspired by the classic restaurants of Europe but transnational in their mixing and matching of certain dishes to meet American tastes). A pioneer of international restaurant consulting who managed some of the best restaurants in the United States, Lang was also a notorious self-promoter; according to one story, when manager of New York City's famous

[86] Barry, *Femininity in Flight*, 108.

Four Seasons restaurant a customer suggested to him that he needed no lessons in hubris. 'Of course not,' Lang reputedly replied, 'It's a Middle Eastern dip, and I know it perfectly well.'[87] While business connections undoubtedly played a part in influencing this positive review, the endorsement served as confirmation that Pan Am's first-class food service still aspired to the fine dining standards that had characterized the partnership with Maxim's.

By the 1980s, however, and with transitions in the industry, the exclusive partnership with Maxim's was becoming a distant memory. The company now dealt with several suppliers and caterers, with the airline's catering centres managed by different companies. The first point of contact between a Pan Am employee and a supplier now occurred much later: in the counting of meals and beverages by flight attendants prior to take-off.[88] The functions of the commissary department had largely been streamlined into Pan Am's dining services department, a small team of just 17 people who managed galley and equipment design, the development of menu specifications, scheduling, loading plans, food selection, pricing, caterer selections and field support. In dealing with its caterers, the company adhered to the long-standing goal of developing major menus locally, using local talent and local produce. Yet whereas the issue of food safety liability and standardized product once sat squarely with the airline, liability was now spread across a number of different companies.[89] Ultimately, however, Pan Am still had the greater brand liability to consider should something go awry and so periodically, and in line with this concern, the airline's contracted caterers from across the world were invited to its Miami headquarters for conferences and discussions hosted by the dining services department. Although the airline had by this point diversified its catering supply, the economies of scale remained staggering, with a one cent mistake in a caterer's price for an individual item such as silver forks or plastic cups easily building up to tens or hundreds of thousands of dollars over time if left unchecked. But while the company's trademark characteristics such as the roast tenderloin of beef remained firmly in place, the company was increasingly focused on cost-cutting.[90] While the fusion of the sometimes fusty Old World formalities with modern practices remained, the profit-driven imperatives of an increasingly saturated market were, for Pan Am, slowly killing its fine dining ideal and, in the end, heightening the dreaded sense of anachronism.

---

[87] *New York Times*, 22 April 1998; 'Clipper 83 named best meal service in 1986', *Clipper* (January/February 1987), 2.

[88] Susan Timper, 'Catering to customer expectations', *Clipper* (November 1990), 4.

[89] Erica Sheward, *Aviation Food Safety* (Oxford: Blackwell, 2006), 12.

[90] Susan Timper, 'The dining services department: Doing what they do best', *Clipper* (July–August 1989).

4

The Crew's perspective: Training, eating and service

Nautical glamour: Pan Am's early employees as sailors

As this book has argued, the often-overlooked aspect behind airline food was the sense of entertainment, surprise and glamour previously associated with dining on the high seas. Trippe was a Navy man, having received his training in the US Navy's First World War air corps, and from the beginning, as we have seen, linked his fleet of aircraft to the luxury ocean liners, including terminology, design and service. As the *New York Times* asked of the dining experience on the Clippers, 'was it a plane, a ship, or a restaurant?'[1] Such pleasantly bemusing ambiguity was exactly what Trippe wanted. When First Lady Eleanor Roosevelt christened the *Yankee Clipper* in 1939 it was in the traditional manner in which ships were launched – with the breaking of a champagne bottle over its bow. In a ceremony carefully choreographed by the company, Mrs Roosevelt first poured a drop to posterity, to 'the glory that was the sailing clippers', before doing the honours.[2] But the links with nautical glamour went further than the image of the First Lady breaking bubbly over the nose of a boat-shaped airplane. Betty Trippe wrote of the majesty of her honeymoon cruise with Juan aboard the SS *Rotterdam*, a slow steamer from New York to Southampton where everyone dressed for dinner each night, the ladies always appearing in a different gown, followed by dancing accompanied by a fine orchestra. The return trip was aboard the SS *Bremen*, a German steamer which featured a Ritz restaurant on the upper deck.[3] From the earliest days of his operation, then, Trippe sought to recreate this atmosphere, aiming to create the ocean liner of the air, including the best of food service.

---

[1] *New York Times*, 'The 30th anniversary of the first China Clipper', 21 November 1965.
[2] Pan Am press release, 27 February 1939. University of Miami special collections, Pan Am collection no. 341, series I, box 106, folder 7.
[3] Trippe, *The Diary and Letters*, 13.

In December 1937, at his request, a communiqué was sent to the eight leading aircraft manufacturers requesting bids on a proposed plane with a pressurized cabin, 'stateroom accommodation' for at least a hundred passengers and with a dressing room, dining room and galley large enough to prepare, store and serve food 'comfortably.' The specifications proved ahead of their time, though, with several manufacturers submitting preliminary sketches which were turned down by Pan Am's engineers as unfeasible.[4]

Something approximating to such ocean liner specifications arrived with the Boeing B-314 *Clipper* (1939). Much of the nostalgia around Pan Am's food service is surely because, as studies have shown, sharing the experience of eating enhances people's enjoyment of that which is being consumed.[5] While eating in the air has become largely a solitary activity, in the past it was a collective experience. Thus, on the B-314, men's and ladies' bathrooms and dressing rooms were placed at opposite ends of the fuselage, providing not only gender separation but also the spectacle of patrons coming to the main cabin dressed for dinner, like on the great passenger liners (although the location of the men's bathroom opposite the galley occasionally created an unfortunately malodorous mix, a reminder that the unglamorous underbelly of airline food service was the collection of waste in vast holding tanks aboard the plane).[6] The oceanic link continued to be stressed into the 1960s, when menus regularly featured watercolour paintings of the famous Clipper ships of the nineteenth century.

Accordingly, in the early days, the outfits of the stewards providing service reinforced the nautical theme. As photographs of airline food service in the 1930s show, an all-male staff wore outfits comprising black trousers and white waist-length jackets, white shirts with black ties and, on occasion, a white garrison hat.[7] On these early flights, the ocean-going tradition of the senior pilot dining formally with the most important or interesting passenger was practised, with his co-pilot taking the wheel.[8] During and after the Second World War, many airlines adapted their uniforms to the style of the armed forces, with Pan Am sticking firmly to the naval look. In keeping with conservative naval traditions, the company remained behind the curve when it came to female

---

[4] 'History of Pan American World Airways' (1946), University of Miami special collections, Pan Am collection no. 341, series I, box 196, folder 10.

[5] E. J. Boothby, M. S. Clark and J. A. Bargh, 'Shared experiences are amplified', *Psychological Science* 25 (2014), 2209–16.

[6] Presland, 'The system of the flying clippers', 29.

[7] Lawrence Mahoney, *The Early Birds: A History of Pan Am's Clipper Ships* (Miami: Pickering Press, 1987), 49.

[8] Dunning, *Voices of My Peers*, 134.

recruitment: while many American airlines had recruited women by 1935, Pan Am persisted with an all-male steward staff until the mid-1940s, reflecting the European tradition of restaurant high dining with food delivered by male waiters.[9] In the early days, and consistent with the sexist norms of the age, the physical demands of Clipper flights over long distances were considered 'too strenuous' for women.[10] Most stewards were aged under 30 and were trained in cooking, serving and even how to survive on an island in case of emergency, including what food to eat and what not to eat. They were referred to somewhat dismissively in an early in-house history as 'flight butlers and general factota' but they would become, as the history admitted, 'one of the most highly praised features of Pan American service'.[11]

The first eight female flight attendants, or hostesses, were hired by United Airlines in 1930 but female flight attendants did not become the norm across the industry until later in the following decade, with international carriers like Air France commencing female recruitment in 1946. When female flight attendants were recruited en masse in the late 1940s, the legacy of ocean liner service was emphasized: they travelled on merchant seaman's passports, combined the functions of a purser and steward like on liners, and received specialist training in the preparation and serving of food.[12] Perhaps recalling fondly his honeymoon, Trippe's penchant for the marine motif continued right into the jet age. A lead engineer of the Boeing 747 got the distinct impression that 'Pan Am's chairman wanted the new Boeing 747 to be an aerial ocean liner, with tall sides punctuated by two parallel rows of windows like portholes. If he had his way, passengers viewing the 747 from the airport terminal would look out and see something suggestive of a ship'.[13] Female in-flight fashion was an integral part of service, too, and the Pan Am uniform underwent several changes, although the maritime blue was always retained. In the 1940s stewardesses wore blouses, caps and a pleated skirt which fell a very proper three inches below the knee; by 1959 and the arrival of the jet age the company recruited Beverly Hills couturier Don Loper, who remodelled the uniform into a torso-length four-button jacket and skirt; and with the coming of the 747 in the 1970s flight attendant uniforms

[9] Victoria Vantoch, *The Jet Sex: Airline Stewardesses and the Making of an American Icon* (Philadelphia: University of Pennsylvania Press, 2013), 25.

[10] Trautman, *Pan American Clipper*, 226.

[11] 'History of Pan American World Airways' (1946), University of Miami special collections, Pan Am collection no. 341, series I, box 196, folder 10.

[12] *New Horizons*, July–September 1945, University of Miami special collections, Pan Am collection no. 341, series I, box 291, folder 10.

[13] Sutter, *747: Creating the World's First Jumbo Jet and Other Adventures from a Life in Aviation*, 88.

were designed by Frank Smith of the women's wear company Evan-Picone, which featured a gold jumper and blue top-skirt with matching jacket. By this stage the skirts had risen to a more daring two inches above the knee.[14] By the standards of the age – which saw female flight attendants at competitor airlines serve food while dressed in revealing hot pants – Pan Am's uniforms continued to conform to the conservative standards of the naval tradition. Yet the Evan-Picone designs also included a 'French butcher's apron' for food service; made of white polyester cotton with pockets in blue, the apron with its large patch pockets was introduced to ease in-flight food service (Figure 4.1).[15] As airline food grew more refined, the role of the female employee duly transitioned from sailor to housewife.

Steward(ess)ing

If Pan Am forced its employees to adhere to the military conformity of naval service, then food service often provided an opportunity for employees to break free of such rigidities and occupy alternative roles. Pan Am pioneered the showing of in-flight movies in 1946, but the emphasis remained on the flight attendant providing entertainment as part of the service. One renowned male flight attendant of the 1970s gained popularity by putting on an illuminated rotating bow tie and treating the customers to flamboyant food service. Such was his entertainment value that – like in the early days of flying with one's favourite purser – passengers would request further flights with him when booking.[16] Another 1970s favourite among Pan Am passengers and staff alike was the redoubtable Zoe Hirschfeld, who is recalled fondly by many former employees. Hirschfeld was a stoutly built woman with a sharp and sassy manner, marking her out as atypical in her peer group. Her curt style won her some enemies but many admirers. Former colleagues recall an occasion where, struggling under the weight of the maximum number of food trays staff were allowed to carry (six) an impatient passenger thrust another dirty tray on top. Hirschfeld is said to have responded 'thank you, sir; now wait a moment while I stick a broom up my ass and sweep the galley too'.[17]

[14] Memo on in-flight fashion, University of Miami special collections, Pan Am collection no. 341, series I, box 291, folder 10.
[15] 'French Butcher's Apron', University of Miami special collections, Pan Am collection no. 341, series I, box 292, folder 9.
[16] Email correspondence with Bryony Holding, 15 January 2018.
[17] Interview with several members of World Wings International Miami chapter, 15 March 2018.

Figure 4.1 Stewardess in Evan-Picone apron. Courtesy: University of Miami Library Special Collections.

The theatricality of the steward or stewardess's role was a throwback to the performance expected of the hotel waiter in the previous century and the terminology bears consideration. Early male flight staff occupying a senior role were sometimes interchangeably referred to as 'pursers' and 'stewards'. When female recruitment became usual, pursers could be male or female, but until the 1970s the less senior flight attendant was almost always female: a female steward, or 'stewardess'. Illustrative of the demanding nature of the role, the term derived from the steward of the great Victorian hotels, an important employee who was senior to waiting staff and expected to be simultaneously a quasi-butler, a storekeeper, a cook, a meat-cutting, wine-serving, money-handling, kitchen-governing man of action.[18]

Yet the role of the flight stewardess went beyond the demanding role of the old hotel steward or adhering to conservative maritime appearances. For Pan Am, the jet age brought with it the intertwining of corporate objectives, normative gender roles and the cultural struggle of the Cold War. The 'stewardess' was now a cultural ambassador, an ideal of American femininity and a glamour girl: a key reason why the antics of the acerbic Zoe Hirschfeld, who stands out as an anomaly, are remembered so keenly by former employees. While the company increasingly recruited younger and slimmer female flight attendants throughout the 1950s and 1960s (a company missive of the time instructed that female staff should be 'of course, attractive') Pan Am resisted the outright eroticization of the air stewardess, insisting on a more understated appearance and uniform than competitor airlines.[19] When these gender roles are considered in the light of food service, some contradictory trends emerge. While embodying a globe-trotting and breezy cosmopolitanism, Pan Am stewardesses also represented American domesticity, and food service was integral to this role, as evidenced in marketing material of the era, where the Pan Am stewardess was at times represented as a mother figure and at other times as an object of desire. To quote a company press release from 1957, the Pan Am stewardess was not only 'a pretty, cheerful girl who can open a bottle of champagne' but also a maternal caregiver who 'can prepare a baby's bottle'. In line with the expectations of the age, the average career of a stewardess at this time was two years and 90 per cent of resignations were for one reason: marriage.[20] The implication was clear: food service in the air was a traineeship for food service at home as a housewife. For female employees, opportunities for self-expression outside the semi-militarised norms of the company were therefore confined by sexist expectations of a woman's role.

---

18 See A. K. Sandoval-Strauss, *Hotel: An American History* (New Haven, CT: Yale University Press, 2007); Jefferson Williamson, *The American Hotel: An Anecdotal History* (New York: Knopf, 1930), 202.

19 Vantoch, *The Jet Sex*, 114–82.

20 Dick Logan, 'The Stewardesses' Story', University of Miami special collections, Pan Am collection no. 341, series I, box 292, folder 13.

'Mother Cooks'

Although marriage frequently signalled the end of a stewardess's working life, it is important to note that Pan Am was unique among US carriers in allowing women who married to continue working if they wished. Undoubtedly, the option to continue service was countered by considerable social pressure (from husbands, fellow employees or managers) that female employees stop working upon marriage, but by the conservative standards of the 1950s this was a relatively enlightened policy. What was insisted upon, however, was that women who were pregnant had to cease working.

In the eyes of the company, stewardesses expecting a baby had already received the perfect training in the caring maternal role. An archetypal account of this link was written very shortly after Pan Am recruited female staff. In 1944, Pan Am flight attendant Louise Taylor penned a special article for *The Woman* magazine detailing a stressful food service:

> I was having 21 guests for lunch that day, including the children and the chaplain. The most reverend gentleman had arrived rather unexpectedly and already was beginning to harrumph in full diaphragm as if to suggest that it was well beyond his customary mealtime. Colonel K. was roaring for American cigarettes and the nice-looking young Englishman had brought along a bottle of pisco and was insisting I join him in 'just one quick one' … the baby was squalling to high heaven … Harassing, you say? … how would you like to cope with it single handed – sans cook, sans maid, sans nurse – in the close confines of a Pan American Clipper high above the Caribbean? Take my word for it, girls, it's nowhere near so bad as it sounds.

Of course, Taylor's experience as a flight attendant had prepared her perfectly for food service on the ground. She was one of the first flight attendants hired by Pan Am and explained to readers of *The Woman* magazine how her experience in the air had given her a perfect template for food service in the home. If feeling stressed at home, she just thought back to her Clipper days:

> The baby's bottle had reached the proper temperature the precise instant the child awakened screaming … from the steam table in the galley luncheon could be served on time and with a flourish. The Chaplain, having done justice to the sole and bisque tortoni, relaxed with a thin black cigar between his fingers and eyed his coffee with the utmost affection. A few words with the young English engineer about the genesis of pisco, that pungent Peruvian brandy, were enough

to launch him into a eulogy on South American wines, in which he was joined by the Chilean diplomat across the way.[21]

Pan Am's female flight attendants were 'just like mother cooks', claimed another female-authored article of the era, this time from the *Washington Post*, and it was 'fun to watch the stewardess serve twenty-one dishes from her kitchenette in less than an hour, as you skim past gorgeous scenery, and soft, billowy clouds'.[22] The message was reiterated in 1950, with the Pan Am stewardess represented as a housewife par excellence. 'Could Mrs. Average American Housewife prepare, cook and serve meals to 69 persons?' asked a company press release. 'Could she do it three times a day and in between meals serve cocktails and snacks? Could she do it in a space with little more room than a good-sized household closet? The answer? She could not. Yet this is precisely what Pan American Airways expects of its stewardesses.'[23]

Food technology also affected the role. The aluminium tray of the airline meal, and the efficient oven in which it was heated, presaged the emergence of the archetypal American housewife of the 1950s. As well as weight saving, the use of new items and devices in airplane kitchens – like in home kitchens – saved time, making the chores of the kitchen easier and faster. Promoted as a way to free women from the drudgery of food preparation and other housework, it promised an era of easy cuisine. Part of a wider movement towards scientific efficiency in food preparation, such changes were tied to the logistics revolution which, in turn, revolutionized the notion of the restaurant itself by delivering 'fast food' drive-through restaurants.[24] Beyond merely aiding the housewife, some early feminist writers argued that the discovery of these new materials and the consequent labour efficiency in the kitchen would change not just the physical world but the world of gender relations. Other progressive writers of the early twentieth century imagined a future in which the preparation of the family meal would itself be a thing of the past; instead the efficiencies, economies of scale and positive social benefits of *communal dining* would deliver the adult female from having to slave over a stove. The notion is intriguing when one considers the hundreds of people fed during airline meal service, particularly on the great 747s. Although operating in a privatized and elitist environment,

[21] Louise Taylor, 'Stewardess Story in first person', *The Woman*, 22 May 1944.
[22] Martha Ellyn, '160 mile airline meals good to the last mile', *Washington Post*, 25 July 1941.
[23] 'Mile-High Kitchen' (1950), University of Miami special collections, Pan Am collection no. 341, series I, box 108, folder 3.
[24] Mimi Sheller, *Aluminium Dreams: The Making of Light Modernity* (Cambridge, MA: MIT Press, 2014), 14.

the flight attendant fed people en masse; airline meal service was thus, in its distinct way, a form of social eating, with over four hundred people being served at the same time. For all the technical progress promising broader social change, however, the Pan Am flight attendant was fundamentally represented as wifely.

By the 1960s, things had changed little, as spelled out in a company press release from 1963:

> There are generally job openings in the stewardess ranks because the turnover is high – about forty per cent a year. Cupid, apparently, is an inveterate traveller. About 99 per cent of all stewardesses who quit do so to get married. 'Why not' observes one of the glamor college instructors. 'By the time we get through training them they can cook and serve a meal for forty people, they know the proper wines and how to serve them, they're experts at talking to all kinds of people, they know how to take care of children. This is a perfect wife.'[25]

The sexual and social dynamics underpinning the 'high turnover' of flight attendants are illustrated by the fact that for some flight attendants bagging a rich husband was the main object of their employment, with food service providing a perfect opportunity to strike up conversation. One former purser recalled a flight attendant known affectionately as 'Captain's Girl' because she only accepted dinner invitations from pilots or wealthy passengers. Before each flight staff were issued with a confidential VIP list, which she would study assiduously, scanning through it for royals or company executives, whom she would then fawn over during the initial drinks service. Next on her checklist was to scan for wedding rings. This took place during the main food service and, if no rings were evident, she would take a good look at the ring finger to ensure that there was no indentation or lighter coloured skin, an indication that the affluent passenger had merely removed his band.[26]

Pan Am's 1950s promotional material stressed that passengers could enjoy 'all the comforts of your own living room', picturing a man reclining in an armchair with a scotch and a cigarette, a dog sleeping at his feet, and another blowing smoke rings in the shape of hearts at a pretty stewardess. Flying in a Stratocruiser was like experiencing 'an armchair in the clouds' and an ashtray was even built into the arm of the seat. Once again, the flight attendant was depicted as both an object of sexual desire and a domestic carer, depicted in cartoon form in brochures as not only blushing in front of male passengers but also sewing up

---

[25] 'Tower of Babel Builders Never Got Off the Ground', 1 July 1963. University of Miami special collections, Pan Am collection no. 341, series I, box 291, folder 5. Original emphasis.
[26] Frahm, *Above and Below the Clouds*, 131.

Figure 4.2 New recruits, 1960s. Courtesy: Winnie Omodt.

a hole in a child's pants.[27] The not-so-subtle implication was also that the male passenger (for most passengers were still male) could also avail of the services of an in-flight wife. In the 1960s the company went so far as to compare its global gastronomic mission to that of a housewife, describing its job as 'like that of a good housekeeper, who goes to market to feed the family the best way possible on a certain budget' and 'follows the seasons, buying food when it is plentiful, at its best and at the lowest cost'.[28]

Youth, beauty, sex and food

The same sexualized and yet socially conservative conceptions of what constituted the ideal stewardess are to be found in the notes attached to the hiring of female staff (Figure 4.2). By the 1960s these roles were restricted to 21- to 27-year-old single female high school graduates with a proficiency in one language in addition to English and in good physical shape. Factors such as 'posture', 'appearance' and 'good moral character' were supposed to be ancillary concerns, and yet one document, from 1960, details how applicants were turned down for the following reasons:

---

[27] 'Flying Clipperwise' (1951), University of Miami special collections, Pan Am collection no. 341, series I, box 108, folder 14.

[28] 'Preparation of Gourmet Food' (undated), University of Miami special collections, Pan Am collection no. 341, series I, box 292, folder 5.

- 'plain, unattractive'
- 'divorced – has child'
- 'cold, passive'
- 'too much eye makeup'
- 'dumpy – head too small for body'
- 'judo handshake'

Conversely, applicants were favoured for being:

- 'homely'
- 'lady-like'
- 'a pretty girl, pleasant'
- 'friend of [company executive]'
- 'darling personality'[29]

It would appear that Pan Am managers' conception of the ideal flight attendant was closely tied to the 'pretty girl'/'perfect wife' expectations of the food server as outlined above and in line with American post-war expectations of the female role. One former flight attendant recalled that the former was the chief consideration of one of her interviewers, who groped her breasts and rear during the hiring process; she was assured that this was normal procedure 'to make sure you are slender enough for the job'.[30] In line with notions of glamour dating back to Maxim's managers strategically placing pretty young women at the French restaurant's window tables, the company wanted youth and beauty. That Pan Am possessed restricted ideas about gender roles is demonstrated in the fact that it ceased hiring male flight attendants in the 1950s and, although a handful of male pursers were recruited thereafter, it was not until 1972 and an era of various lawsuits against the company on the grounds of discrimination that the appointment of stewards resumed. In the intervening years the women's movement and organized labour had challenged the post-war ideal of female domesticity on which airline food service was largely built and, meanwhile, the so-called sexual revolution had swept across American society.

Keen to portray itself as an enlightened company, Pan Am heralded the re-emergence of the steward as signalling that customer service, regardless of

[29] Pan Am interview notes, Monday 22nd (exact date not listed) 1960, Pan Am collection no. 341, series I, box 291, folder 9.

[30] Interview with Margie Thompson, 15 March 2018. For detailed discussion of the sexist culture of the airline industry at the time also see *Georgia Painter Nielsen, From Sky Girl to Flight Attendant: Women and the Making of a Union* (New York: Cornell University Press, 1982); Kathleen Barry, *Femininity in Flight: A History of Flight Attendants* (Durham, NC: Duke University Press, 2007); Phil Tierneyer, *Plane Queer: Labor, Sexuality, and AIDS in the History of Male Flight Attendants* (Oakland: University of California Press, 2013).

sex, was paramount. The only subject where men and women were instructed separately was in grooming and this, according to the company, was all about ensuring food safety. Male staff, like females, received tips on the care of skin and hands to prevent the dryness and flaking of skin caused by the zero-humidity atmosphere of the pressurized aircraft cabin. 'Fairly long' hairstyles were permitted, but only if 'layered' so as not to interfere with 'the hygienic serving of food'; for the same reason moustaches were deemed acceptable whereas 'beards and mutton-chop sideburns' were not. Food safety also intertwined with sexuality. The return of the male flight attendant was followed by the AIDS crisis of the 1980s. With the nature of infection still uncertain, the airline reassured passengers that all food was handled by employees wearing gloves.[31]

The professionalism of food service

In common with the traditionally militaristic training of hotel waiters, keeping up appearances remained a central aspect of airline food service. Similarly, given the centrality of food service to the Pan Am experience, some company recruiters would select employees based on seemingly small details such as the physical appearance of their hands. One recalled 'I used to look at their hands because, you know, you serve people with trays. I used to look at their hands to see if they were nice. Not necessarily all manicured, but nice.'[32] No one likes to find a hair in their food, and this concern constantly loomed over in-flight service. Instructions issued to staff in the 1980s emphasized that hair products were 'magnets to debris in the air' and attendants were advised to dilute their shampoo to ensure their hair was rinsed properly; the same applied to male gels and mousses, with the 'wet look' not authorized in uniform; hot rollers and curlers should be used with care to ensure that the hair was not 'baked' and minimize the risk of loose strands; for the same reason 'wash and wear' permed hairstyles were also banned. Once again, instructions about hairstyles may have been couched in the language of food safety, but other corporate anxieties were also evident: 'blond hair should not appear "brassy"'; 'to achieve a truly professional image, our true goal should be to enhance our own natural qualities, not change them.'[33] Clearly, and despite changes reflecting broader social transitions,

---

[31] 'Boys and girls together at Pan Am school', Pan Am collection no. 341, series I, box 292, folder 9.
[32] Christine Reiko Yano, *Airborne Dreams: 'Nisei' Stewardesses and Pan American World Airways* (Durham, NC: Duke University Press, 2011), 78.
[33] Pan Am Monthly operational bulletin, vol. 18, no. 6, July 1988, University of Miami digital collections, Pan Am material.

the traditionalism and quasi-militarism of the company persisted. This was underlined when new rules were introduced to make the purser's uniform more authoritative, making it resemble more closely the traditional naval outfit of the plane's captain. In the 1980s the company instructed that the gold stripes on the purser's jacket be widened to project greater visibility and authority; however unpleasantly warm it became in the cabin the purser, unlike flight attendants, was also now prohibited from removing his or her (the purser role remained all-male until 1960) jacket.[34]

The above aspects of food service were underpinned by a rigorous training process. Inspired by moves in the 1930s by German carrier Lufthansa, Pan Am became the second airline in the world to require its staff to undertake culinary training. This requirement was based on an early realization that in-flight food service was crucial in determining passenger opinion and integral to Pan Am's aim for superlative service. Basic flight attendant training took six weeks (two weeks' emergency training and four weeks' service training). The latter covered food preparation, knowledge of wines and champagne, and the composition of various cocktails as well as courses in simple dietetics and table service. Flight attendants received regular awareness courses to ensure they kept abreast of the quality products sourced by Pan Am and how best to handle them.[35] They also undertook training on wines and wine terminology.[36] In the International Training Center (based primarily in Miami, but also in New York and San Francisco) there was a full working mock-up galley and passenger seats where trainees prepared and served cuisine for volunteers, all under the watchful eyes of instructors (Figure 4.3). The volunteers could be family members or partners, who often enjoyed the chance to receive pampered food service. Prior to the mock-up, trainees had to practice serving using the 'spoon and fork technique' (serving while holding a silver spoon and fork in one hand). This was followed by in-flight training in cooking and serving techniques.[37] On occasion, additionally, the company would hire wine experts to come through the first-class cabin offering free tastings and explanations of various wines.[38] A company press release from 1963 was unequivocal in emphasizing the transnational cultural capital gained through its training programme in food service, claiming 'the girl who started the course with the foggy idea that you put a grape in a martini

[34] Pan Am Monthly operational bulletin, Monthly operational bulletin, vol. 16, no. 3, March 1986, University of Miami digital collections, Pan Am material.
[35] Berman, 'Pan Am's Haute Cuisine: Praised to the High Heavens', 7.
[36] Email correspondence with Debbi Fuller, 11 January 2018.
[37] Interview with Dian Groh, 12 January 2018.
[38] Email correspondence with Barbara Sharfstein, 15 January 2018.

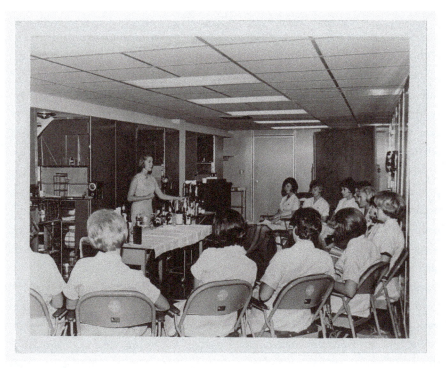

Figure 4.3 Pan Am's International Training Center, Miami, 1960s. Courtesy: University of Miami Library Special Collections.

comes out of it decanting dinner wines and popping champagne corks with the aplomb of a Paris wine steward'.[39]

Although coloured by rose-tinted recollection and company propaganda, the attention to detail included in Pan Am's training around food and drink is of justifiable renown. Take, for instance, the following dialogue in the company's in-house bulletin:

Anonymous staff query:

Could you please give us some information about the pink champagne we serve in first class?

Response by Carlos Bragado, Director, Dining Services:

Champagne rosé, the most expensive in every category of Champagne, is back in vogue as the ultimate Champagne and drink of romance and celebration. It is a beverage steeped in history, relatively rare and difficult to find outside major

[39] 'Tower of Babel Builders Never Got Off the Ground', 1 July 1963. University of Miami special collections, Pan Am collection no. 341, series I, box 291, folder 5.

urban markets. French Moët et Chandon Brut Imperial rosé Vintage is proudly offered in First Class on some premium flights.

Historians say the Champagne rosé phenomenon dates back to 1680 and King Louis XIV, who had a fondness for it. Records suggest that the first Champagne rosé was an accident of nature. No doubt, it was during an unusually hot and sunny summer three centuries ago that the Pinot Noir grapes achieved a greater ripeness causing the pigmentation in the skins to be more concentrated, the fermentation process more rapid, resulting in coloring the juice pale pink before the skins were removed. Exceptional vintages are normally required to produce grapes of this quality. This accounts for the rarity of Champagne rosés today. Only about two percent of total Champagne production consists of Champagne rosé. Fewer than 20,000 bottles of this champagne are imported into the United States each year.

The wine is not marketed until four or five years after it is made. The color was originally described as 'oeuil de perdrix' or 'eye of the partridge'. This suggests a more coppery or salmon tint than does the word rosé. It is also often referred to as 'blush' Champagne. Many feel that the color adds drama and a sense of expectation not as readily imparted by golden Champagnes.[40]

In addition to such extensive education on individual drinks and dishes, each flight attendant's 'Flight Service Handbook' gave detailed instructions on how to conduct service, containing photographs illustrating how items should be arranged on carts and instructions on proper forms of address for distinguished passengers.[41] Staff were pointedly reminded that Pan Am customers expected 'the professional touch of correct pronunciation' when discussing wines.[42] During the training process flight attendants were required to study the history of food and its relationship to specific territories served by Pan Am. 'We do not try to teach the girls to be cooks,' one manager claimed, 'however we do teach them to appreciate food; to treat it properly and to handle it with care.' This included classes on the provenance of different foodstuffs which impressed on trainees the amount of local labour and expense that went into the preparation of certain foodstuffs, especially sauces. 'They learn that beef is best cooked rare, that pork must be well cooked, and that vegetables lose their color and some of their nutritional value if overcooked.'[43]

---

[40] Pan Am Monthly operational bulletin, vol. 16, no. 3, March 1986, University of Miami digital collections, Pan Am material.
[41] Stirn Groh and Snider Sprecher, 'Dining Aloft', 121–4.
[42] Pan Am Monthly operational bulletin, no. 2, Second Quarter 1989, University of Miami digital collections, Pan Am material.
[43] 'Preparation of Gourmet Food' (undated), University of Miami special collections, Pan Am collection no. 341, series I, box 292, folder 5.

As part of training, emphasis was placed on the flight attendant possessing the culinary ability to 'rustle something up' if the circumstances demanded. Helen Davey (flight attendant 1965–86) recalled an example of when food service provided a challenge to the professional ethos of the Pan Am flight attendant, namely *to bring order out of chaos, and to look good doing it*. Boarding a Boeing 707 for a night flight from JFK to Buenos Aires she was confronted by 350 fresh eggs, buckets of fresh butter, and cartons of fresh cream: breakfast for a hundred people. After preparing 350 fresh scrambled eggs she began to heat them up, only for the captain to announce that bad turbulence was expected:

> We heard the sound of the engines slowing down, and felt the eerie quiet just before we hit one very strong bump. I watched in horror as the shelf lined with pans waiting to be cooked rose up a couple of inches. There I was, holding onto that shelf for dear life, not wanting to lose all those breakfasts. One of the containers slid right off the shelf, spilling all over my uniform and shoes. Despite the apron, I was covered with slimy eggs, but even worse, I started slipping and sliding all over the galley floor.

> Bouncing up and down, I was determined to cook those stupid eggs perfectly, against all odds. Somehow, my fellow flight attendants and I got into a 'zone' and we managed, row after row, to deliver beautiful, fluffy scrambled eggs and sausages. Each dish was topped off by one bright green sprig of parsley, otherwise known as 'Pan Am roses,' because no meal was considered complete without it. My fellow flight attendants and I felt extremely gratified when several passengers made a special trip back to the galley to tell us that it was the most delicious meal they had ever had on an airplane!

> I must have been one sorry sight when I got off the airplane on that beautiful, bright and hot summer morning. I couldn't cover myself up with my overcoat because it was too hot. Eggs encrusted my hair, my uniform, my shoes, and my purse. The feeling of satisfaction, however, is something I've never forgotten. My crew and I had found a way to bring order from chaos, and those eggs had not defeated me, even though a referee might call it a draw: when I arrived at my hotel room and undressed, I had scrambled eggs in my bra![44]

International competitors followed Pan Am's lead in punctilious training, research and development, for example, Air France launched its subsidiary Servair in 1971, a body devoted to research and innovation in airline cuisine. With the outsourcing of many of the company's functions in the 1980s, quality control and quality service took on added significance. The burden of responsibility placed

[44]   Helen Davey, '350 Eggs but who's counting?', *Huffington Post*, 17 July 2011.

upon flight attendants to perform this role duly increased. Due to outsourcing, the flight attendant was now the first point of contact between the caterer and the company; they therefore had to check that all meals, beverages and equipment were on board as indicated in the documents provided by the caterer. Aside from heating the food for the correct time, serving it and cleaning it away, any complaints about food service had to be logged and reported. If mechanical failure or under-stocking prevented passengers from being served food mid-air, flight attendants had to provide passengers with a voucher equal to the value of the meal. If food ran short for any reason, flight attendants were even expected to offer up their own meals to disgruntled passengers.[45] Unsurprisingly, then, in performing food service it was also the flight attendant who bore the brunt of customer dissatisfaction.

Eating on the job

This chapter, which has focused on the crew's experience of food service, now turns to a much under-documented aspect of the history of airline food: the consumption habits of flight attendants themselves. After meal service, it was the turn of crew members to eat. If possible, flight attendants would occupy an empty seat in first class or, failing that, economy and, if possible, they would eat food from the first-class menu. The worst place to consume a meal, one purser recalled, was in the galley itself. Invariably, when just about to start dinner, a passenger would appear, looking for more food or, worse, anxious for a chat. 'Where are you from?', 'how long have you been flying?', and 'have you ever been in a plane crash?' were the most common questions. The best answer, he found, was to smile, take a big bite and chomp slowly to kill time, reflecting, as everyone who has been brought up with an idea of table manners knows, that you don't talk with your mouth full.[46]

Crew members aboard the first trans-Pacific flight in 1935, the so-called China Clipper, munched ravenously on pre-packed sandwiches from plastic bags.[47] A short while later, though, as mentioned earlier, the box lunch had given way to hot food. An overlooked dimension to Pan Am's early Pacific expansion was the reliance on shipped supplies and, often, eating at sea was more hazardous

[45] Timper, 'Catering to customer expectations', 4.
[46] Frahm, *Above and Below the Clouds*, 164.
[47] 'Historic Alameda Flight Recalled', *Alameda Times Star*, 17 November 1965. University of Miami special collections, Pan Am collection no. 341, series I, box 61, folder 7.

than eating in the air, despite the relative discomfort of early airplane travel. Pan Am flight engineer Walter Ziegler recorded in his diary the arduous ordeal of crew eating on the company's exploratory voyage to Honolulu in 1937. Aboard ship in stormy weather, he lamented that whereas air turbulence was usually temporary, the ocean was not so forgiving:

> At meal times we have to tie ourselves to the table. When everyone is seated we pass a line around all the chairs, seize it up tight and hold on with one hand. There are guard boards on the table divided off in about fourteen inch squares, the dishes are placed in them but they still travel – tonight the cream, sugar, salt and pepper were all turned over and mixed in a good batter – the salads were all over the table and one just took a fork, or fingers, and ate off the table cloth. By the latter part of dinner I could stand it no longer so I just stood up and grabbed whatever came by.[48]

In the air, it was a safety imperative that the pilot and co-pilot did not eat the same meal. Pilots consumed their food in the cockpit, separate from other staff. A special meal designated Captain's Choice was sometimes provided, each one from a different catering source.[49] Company regulations also dictated that flight attendants placed meals and beverages in positions which did not interfere with the controls; that, to reduce the risk of spillage, food would come in unbreakable plastic containers; and that no alcohol was permitted in the cockpit.[50] The importance of having the pilots eat different food is illustrated by a serious outbreak of food poisoning on board a Pan Am flight between Copenhagen and New York in 1970. 'Everyone got sick from the shrimp cocktail' recalls one former employee, 'everyone was vomiting uncontrollably – crew, passengers – the entire plane was plastered in sick and the toilets were an absolute mess'. The plane was met at John F. Kennedy airport by an array of ambulances and fire engines. Thankfully, as per protocol, one of the pilots had not eaten the shrimp cocktail that day.[51]

When it came to food, the relationship between pilots and flight attendants was not always smooth. One recalled an old-school pilot, Captain Arthur Duggan, insisting aboard a 707 transatlantic flight that none of the crew eat. Puzzled as to what to do with the food, he then watched in amazement as Duggan radioed

[48] J. Walter Ziegler diary entry, 15 November 1937, University of Miami special collections, Pan Am collection no. 341, series I, box 13, folder 2.
[49] Email correspondence with Louis Berman, 22 January 2018.
[50] Pan Am *Monthly operational bulletin*, vol. 18, no. 7, August 1988, University of Miami digital collections, Pan Am material.
[51] Interview with Joan Nell Bernstein, 15 March 2018.

through to Ireland's Shannon airport and then announced to shocked passengers that they would be making an impromptu and unscheduled stop in Ireland: for breakfast. Instead of eating the pre-prepared flight food, Duggan treated the crew to full Irish breakfasts all round.[52] Shannon, a duty-free port where lavish breakfasts were served on white Irish linen, was a favourite stopover for crew. Yet the patrician attitude of pilots was at times resented by flight crew. Many former flight attendants recall the dislike they felt towards pilots who viewed themselves as 'Sky Gods' and who would complain and occasionally sulk if they did not get the food they had requested.[53] One remembers being so upset with one notorious pilot's persistent bullying attitude that she plotted different ways to give him his comeuppance. Eye drops were in plentiful supply at the time because when smoking was permitted on airplanes flight attendants would have to walk back and forth through a confined space full of thick smoke clouds, which made the eyes burn and made the eye drops a travel essential. Therefore, on one occasion, after suffering what she considered an unfair reprimand, she secretly added her eye drop mixture to the pilot's coffee, which had a strong laxative effect.[54]

A considerable perk of the job was that Pan Am flight attendants ate food prepared for first-class passengers, which was often not the sort of food they were used to at home.[55] One former flight attendant 'grew up in a small Rocky Mountain town on a steady diet of my grandmother's basic home cooking, I had no idea roast beef could be served rare, that green beans were not supposed to be grey and that fish eggs were anything more than bait my grandfather used to catch trout'.[56] Another recalled putting on weight after sampling the fresh rolls Pan Am served: 'the flavor was so much more delicious than I was used to, as was the practice of seven courses in first class'.[57] Interestingly, no Pan Am staff recalled that the taste of the food was impaired by altitude, to them it was simply 'scrumptious'.[58] A Pan Am stewardess of the 1980s recalled eating 'a lot of really great cheese, as much caviar as I could salvage, a lot of beef tenderloin, and bits and pieces of whatever else was left over including sacher torte [Viennese chocolate cake]'.[59] She affirmed that altitude did not impair the taste of the food

---

[52] Dunning, *Voices of My Peers*, 212.
[53] Interview with Sybille Holder, 15 March 2018.
[54] Interview with Donna Valdes, 15 March 2018.
[55] Email correspondence with Jerry Holmes, 10 January 2018.
[56] Interview with Teresa Webber, 18 January 2018.
[57] Interview with Dian Groh, 12 January 2018.
[58] Interview with Dian Groh, 12 January 2018.
[59] Email correspondence with Debbi Fuller, 10 January 2018.

and was typical of many flight attendants in that she was 'completely unaware of a lot of the cuisines of the world' before joining Pan Am. She recalls:

> I had never eaten caviar but was thrilled to discover that I LOVED it. We served it two ways, one in the Russian style with blinis [pancakes] and sour cream and the more traditional way with chopped egg white, chopped egg yolk and chopped onion. Both types were served with small glasses of chilled vodka. I once finished the fairly generous remnants of an entire tin of Beluga caviar when it came back to the galley and we were close to landing. I didn't want it to go to waste … these days, I am happy to eat pretty much any cuisine you can name! I have Pan Am to thank for that![60]

Many developed a culinary wanderlust borne of developing transnational tastes. One flight attendant would pick her flights dependent on the on-board food, which Pan Am always matched with the country travelled to, relishing the memory of 'the best gravlax ever' on the Oslo flight and the 'creamiest, best cheeses served in First Class from Paris'.[61] Another employee recalled how training in Cordon Bleu hospitality broadened her culinary horizons and made her more adventurous in her own kitchen: 'You had to follow a standard and the level of expectation was very high … I was exposed to so much all over the world as far as food and drink are concerned [that] at home I cook a lot more multicultural than if I had stayed at home.'[62] Christmas was always an occasion for cultural exchange around food; to accompany dinner and overcome homesickness, cabin crew working on Christmas Day would produce Christmas titbits from around the world – whether paper napkins emblazoned with *Feliz Navidad* or German gingerbread and marzipan – and the galley itself would often be converted into a lavishly decorated, multicultural Christmas grotto.[63] Beluga caviar was the favourite of many a flight attendant. One recalled in detail the dainty set-up for serving this delicacy – 'on crisp white or blue linen with small bowls of creme fraiche, finely diced onion, egg yolks and egg whites, thin slices of lemon, Melba toast and well-chilled bottles of vodka and champagne. The tin of caviar always took centre stage on a bed of ice within a large silver tureen.' So coveted among staff was the Caspian's black gold that, despite the fraught diplomatic relations between the United States and Iran following the 1979 revolution, on a layover in Iran she undertook the potentially hazardous

---

[60] Email correspondence with Debbi Fuller, 11 January 2018.
[61] Wendy Knecht, 'The joy of world class cuisine', *New York Lifestyles Magazine* 2, 6 (June 2016).
[62] Cited in Reiko Yano, *Airborne Dreams*, 156.
[63] Frahm, *Above and Below the Clouds*, 188.

task of venturing into the marketplaces of downtown Tehran to procure some for herself. Her bartering tool was 'two bottles of Johnny Walker Scotch whiskey, which we'd purchased at our previous port in Hong Kong for $5 a bottle'. She recalls that the officers of Tehran Customs, in searching crew bags, were more desirous of fondling lingerie or confiscating playing cards than seizing alcohol and so, armed with the whisky, she took a taxi to the local fish market, eventually exchanging the alcohol for an enormous container of caviar.[64]

Yet there was a more insidious side to the delights of sampling fine foods on the job. After being hired, female flight attendants were given 'weight maximums', which were determined by height, and could be put on the scales when reporting for briefings; if the maximum was exceeded during employment it resulted in more regular 'weight checks' and, failing improvement, the termination of employment. One female flight attendant recalled how the joy of sampling cherries jubilee and chocolate mousse in first class soon led to weight gain. She attempted to avoid the company's routine weight checks by working night flights (when supervisors were off-duty) but she soon received a 'weight slip' from her grooming supervisor informing her that her weight – 149 pounds – was in excess of her allotted weight as determined by her height – 136 pounds – and that she was now required to attend weight checks every two weeks to ensure she was losing the extra.[65] Another former flight attendant recalled how 'the weight check thing was a constant source of terror for us. Yikes! We did have to be careful. I was from the American South, and we had a terrible diet where I grew up.' She managed to overcome the almost inevitable weight gain by 'watching the European girls on the plane and how they ate. They sat down, they enjoyed a good meal, and they didn't snack.'[66]

Staff were also required to wear girdles if deemed necessary by a manager. The frequency of weight checks appears to have varied per location, with some former staff recalling weekly checks and others maintaining that these occurred at less regular intervals. That weight checks did not always take place on a weekly basis is suggested by the recollections of two former flight attendants who – contrary to company policy – successfully hid their pregnancies for four and six months, respectively.[67] By its latter years, in the wake of the women's movement and a number of lawsuits around the issue, the company was forced to change the policy of weight checks. Pan Am's arm was eventually twisted by

[64] Interview with Teresa Webber, 18 January 2018.
[65] Patricia O'Neill, cited in Vantoch, *The Jet Sex*, 188.
[66] Interview with Rebecca Sprecher, 6 February 2018.
[67] Interview with Margie Thompson and Donna Valdes, 15 March 2018.

actions brought by individuals and the International Union of Flight Attendants (IUFA). In a well-publicized ruling of 1987, the California District Court ruled that the company's policy was in violation of Title VII of the US Civil Rights Act (1964). Pan Am, however, bullishly informed employees that pending the conclusion of supplementary talks with the IUFA, which were ordered by the court in an attempt to reach an agreement, the policy remained in place 'in its entirety', warning 'any flight attendant currently on a weight reduction program must continue to meet all the requirements of the program'.[68] To the end, the Pan Am ideal of the glamourous stewardess was tied to the body beautiful.

The high life

When it came to alcohol, another constant of in-flight consumption, it was the responsibility of the crew to oversee that liquor kits were locked and that the customs seal was intact. Liquor was held in the bond (with no customer access) and monitored by customs at airports. Flight attendants could not open the liquor kits until after take-off, so to overcome this Pan Am offered a pre-departure drink of champagne on which duty had been paid.[69] Crew were, of course, forbidden from drinking on duty but, as one former flight attendant recalled, 'we developed artful ways to plug open bottles of champagne and smuggle them through customs to consume at our crew parties'.[70] Smuggling alcohol was a time-honoured company tradition. Hank Anzohler of the maintenance division remembers staff being temporarily stationed in the US Marine base at Pearl City, Hawaii, during the Second World War. There, Pan Am staff would smuggle in whisky beneath the noses of Marine guards by transferring it into soda bottles. One of his colleagues even cut a hole in the perimeter fence of the base to greater facilitate his alcohol smuggling, leading to a panicked investigation by the Marines into possible Japanese spy activity.[71] After champagne was introduced to flights in the 1940s a strict 'champagne check system' operated to guard against theft. After serious discrepancies arose, Tony Olanio – Pacific/Alaska division chief – launched a personal investigation, only to find out about a concerted attempt among staff to stockpile champagne.

---

[68] Pan Am Monthly operational bulletin, vol. 17, no. 5, May 1987, University of Miami digital collections, Pan Am material.
[69] Interview with Barrie Fewster, 23 January 2018.
[70] Email correspondence with Rebecca Sprecher, 18 January 2018.
[71] Dunning, *Voices of My Peers*, 66.

But since the object of the theft, he learned, was to squirrel away dozens of champagne bottles for a big crew party to mark the wedding of two employees he decided to turn a blind eye.[72] From the recollections of flight crew, it is clear that the moderate consumption of champagne was viewed as a harmless perk of the job which may have infringed the letter, but not the spirit, of the law. Purser Harry Frahm's first flight aboard the Stratocruiser in the 1950s was also his first introduction to in-flight drinking. While a female flight attendant nonchalantly filled two paper cups with Moët and Chandon, handing him one, he stammered 'but … we are not allowed to drink alcoholic beverages in uniform'. 'Fine!', she bellowed in reply, and leant down, undid his shoelaces and removed his shoe. 'One shoe off! now you are out of uniform!'[73]

While the hedonism of the airline golden age suggested in marketing and popular culture is overstated, the alluring conviviality of eating and drinking was certainly part of the employee experience. As one flight attendant recalls in her memoirs, 'we had very long layovers in seductive places like Tahiti and Samoa, where the so-called "crew parties" flourished and drinking and dancing and romancing and sex were all part of it'.[74] Others recall sunbathing in destinations such as the Gold Coast, the crew reclining together with picnic baskets full of local delicacies, or dining in exotic destinations such as Rio de Janeiro, frequently with cabin crew from other airlines.[75] Cultural differences between employees affected consumption patterns in leisure times; for example, Japanese-American flight attendants were renowned for their relative abstemiousness.[76] On the other hand, according to a *Wall Street Journal* piece from 1969 which interviewed an anonymous stewardess from a major airline, 'when a flight is rough or overly demanding she will slip into the plane's galley and gulp a Bloody Mary; on occasion she smokes marijuana before a flight and takes her own kind of trip in the air'.[77] Interviews with retired Pan Am flight attendants from the 1960s and 1970s confirm the above story. One recalls making punch for herself and the rest of the flight crew from the leftovers of passengers' drinks: red wine, white wine, orange juice, cognac. Alcohol was also smuggled off aircraft by secreting it in empty coffee urns, orange juice containers or bottles of mouthwash. She would even hide marijuana underneath her hat ribbon.[78] Flight attendants

---

[72] Dunning, *Voices of My Peers*, 122.
[73] Frahm, *Above and Below the Clouds*, 49.
[74] Aimee Bratt, *Glamor and Turbulence – I Remember Pan Am, 1966–91* (New York: Vantage, 1996), 21.
[75] Frahm, *Above and Below the Clouds*, 77.
[76] Reiko Yano, *Airborne Dreams*, 143.
[77] Melodie Bowsher, 'The high life', *Wall Street Journal*, 3 June 1969.
[78] Donna Valdes, interviewed 15 March 2018.

clearly felt like their profession imbued them with a sharp-witted attitude to life's established rules, especially when it came to rules prohibiting the importation or consumption of alcohol. A common saying summarizing flight attendants' transnational savvy was 'we know our way around the world like you know your way around the block'.[79]

Cookbooks

For many employees, the experience of airline food – with both its negative and positive aspects – remained, in retirement, the most treasured memory of working life. Chapters of World Wings International, Pan Am's alumni association founded in 1957, regularly host dinner parties where dining experience at altitude is recreated. There have also been cookbooks featuring recipes collected by retired flight attendants. *The International Hostess Cook Book* appeared in 1972, its tag line 'recipes not lab-tested but love tested'. Published by World Wings International, it featured a washable cover 'for the hostess with a flair for splattering meringue coverings onto everything within reach' and an international flavour, featuring over two hundred recipes from chapter members worldwide.[80] In the foreword, Graham Kerr – known to a generation of American television foodies as the 'Galloping Gourmet', noted that a personal touch was added by the comments accompanying each recipe by the 'hostess' who submitted it. Aided by a strident publicity campaign from the company and an endorsement by First Lady Pat Nixon, the first two thousand copies of the book sold out within weeks. Mrs Nixon, who had christened the first 747 in 1970, implied that she would use recipes in the book to cook for her husband, President Richard Nixon. Not for the first time, a Pan Am venture was receiving the blessing of the political establishment. 'Spaetzle, kuku, kibbeh, frikadeller, manicotti and baba ghannouj may sound like the lyrics of a new song hit or a garbled telegram' one press release announced, 'but in reality they are titles of recipes from a new cookbook'.[81] The volume proved such a success that a second was commissioned, appearing in 1974, with the proceeds from both volumes going to charities patronized by World Wings International (Figure 4.4). In

[79] Ana Lancombe, interviewed 15 March 2018; Sybille Holder, interviewed 15 March 2018.
[80] Diane Casselberry, 'Stewardess Cookbook exotic but practical', University of Miami special collections, Pan Am collection no. 341, series I, box 291, folder 6.
[81] Cook Book press release (undated), University of Miami special collections, Pan Am collection no. 452, series I, box 11, folder 99.

Figure 4.4 Promotional photograph for *The International Hostess Cook Book*, 1972. Courtesy: University of Miami Library Special Collections.

fact the book proved such a hit, particularly among former employees who had gone on to become housewives, that logistical difficulties soon arose around its distribution due to so many members in so many chapters around the world requesting it.[82]

The 1970s cookbooks followed in the wake of Pan Am's first cookbook, Myra Waldo's *Complete Round-the-World Cookbook* of 1954, which was a joint effort between the company and Waldo, a food writer. The book was launched in unique fashion, aboard a Stratocruiser, with assembled members of the press treated to an eclectic selection from the cookbook's pages including Hawaiian salmon, Mexican guacamole, Ecuadorian shrimp, Belgian beef steak, Italian green salad, Burmese coconut rice, Brazilian nut cake and French champagne.[83] Keen to capitalize on the marketing potential derived from the book's international

[82] See University of Miami special collections, Pan Am collection no. 452, series I, box 11, folder 103.

[83] Pan Am press release, 21 October 1954, University of Miami special collections, Pan Am collection no. 341, series I, box 213, folder 14.

flavour, the company aligned itself strongly with the publication, stocking it in every Pan Am office in the United States.

'Whether we like it or not', proclaimed Waldo in the *Round-the-World Cookbook*'s introduction, 'world leadership has come to the United States'. And the book was unashamedly just that: a leadership manual. It sought to broaden the horizons of average Americans to 'the world of travel, the observation of the life and ways of others, the spirit of inquiry' and – perhaps the greatest challenge of all – 'the willingness to eat what others eat'. Containing over six hundred global recipes gathered from local hotels, restaurants, gourmets and employees in each of the 84 countries Pan Am served, its leitmotif was stridently globalizing and transnational, driving the gastronomic 'maturity' of the United States and urging readers to consider that 'in this atomic age our neighbors *are* the Patagonians, the Zulus, and the people next door'.[84] American 'world leadership' would be transnational and all-embracing and Pan Am, in opening up global culinary vistas to Americans, would be its chief herald.

The use of the term 'world leadership' demonstrated that even in the post-war period, that era of supposedly enlightened American global leadership, the *Complete Round-the-World Cookbook* of 1954 resembled a leadership manual for Americans. Its author, Myra Waldo, was a wealthy globetrotting hostess and the tone and format was, in turn, geared towards exotic titbits of information for use on the New York dinner party scene. Just as Pan Am would churn out guides to every country of the world, every golf course worth playing in the world and the best universities in the world to send your children to, it could capture – in one volume – every dish worth eating in the world. Naturally, Waldo provided a sanitized version for her readers: some recipes were amended to fit American tastes better and spellings were Americanized too. The illustrations provided a juxtaposition: smart Americans in suits and hats boarding Pan Am planes, the natives in extravagant national dress performing outlandish dances. At times, in describing local cuisines and cultures, Waldo's cookbook lent heavily towards the amusement and delectation of the white traveller. For instance, the simplicity of Burmese curries spoke to the fact that they were a 'smiling, trusting people who are unaware of ulcers, the stock market, high blood pressure' and one could recreate Rudyard Kipling's imperial world there through 'dining in the British fashion'; Irish moonshine (poteen) was distilled from potatoes by 'little Irish

---

[84] Myra Waldo, *The Complete Round-the-World Cookbook* (New York: Doubleday, 1954), 8.

leprechauns high up in the hills'; and discussion of African cuisine was mocking, referring to the 'culinary style of the many cannibals who remain there today'.[85]

As the next chapter outlines, many Pan Am customers consequently expected transnational delectation, not just from their food but from their food server. As this chapter has shown, flight attendants were very much the front-line troops in difficult encounters with passengers, particularly when reality fell short of idealistic expectation. Not only was the airline food server supposed to be slim, obliging, knowledgeable, polite, professional and glamourous, but these same qualities assumed racialized and orientalist dimensions consistent with the elitism and imperialism quietly underpinning the pan American ideal. This theme is explored in greater depth in the final chapter, which further examines the company's hiring policy and the experiences of its staff and argues that – rather than representing a new type of imperium – American 'world leadership', as exemplified by Pan Am and its foodways, replicated some of the darker features of Old World colonialism.

[85] Waldo, *The Complete Round-the-World Cookbook*, 226, 86, 212.

5

'Colonizers in the cause of aviation': Geopolitics and the emergence of transnational cuisine

In an age of global mass communication and travel it is easy to overlook the extent to which Pan Am's pioneering routes across the Americas and the Pacific transformed the interconnectivity of people and nations. For example, when it commenced in 1941, the company's semi-monthly flight from San Francisco to Singapore reduced the journey time between the two cities – 8,500 miles apart – from twenty-five days to just six. As the century progressed and technologies improved, flight times continued to fall dramatically. Pan Am's reach ensured it was in the vanguard of transnationalism and globalization, processes whereby the world 'got smaller' and the significance of national boundaries receded.[1] In many ways, then, when passengers stepped into a Pan Am cabin they were stepping into a new nation altogether, or a 'nation of nations' as the company liked to see itself. At a stretch, this was a 'United Nations' experience, with passengers flying under international blue globe emblem and at the service of an internationally diverse staff. Nothing illustrated this better than Pan Am's food service. With culinary offerings from the four corners of the world, passengers could pore over a menu full of choice before sampling nationally eclectic dishes. But in making the local global on its own terms, was the company merely acting as an agent of American colonialism and cultural appropriation?

---

[1] Michael Howard, *Transnationalism: An Introduction* (Jefferson, NC: McFarland, 2011), 28–9.

'Good, plain, wholesome things'

To answer this question, we must return to the company's early days. Dining Pan Am was not initially the transnational utopia of company lore. The evolution of Pan Am's gastronomy was a long process. In the very earliest days the purser may have occasionally shopped locally, but as the company grew in the 1930s and 1940s its cuisine became resolutely American. This was announced unequivocally by the stars and stripes of the early dining cabins designed by Norman Bel Geddes and on the Pan Am services of the 1930s and 1940s, where the dinner menu stuck to American favourites such as shrimp cocktail, turtle soup, and steak and mashed potato, while breakfast was cereal, eggs, bacon, sausages, tea and coffee.[2] The company's fêted '160 Mile Dinner' of the 1940s, which presented dishes at certain distances, did not buck this trend: at 10 miles tomato bisque was served, at 100 fried chicken, at 130 salad, at 150 dessert and at 160 coffee.[3] In essence, 160 miles of American cuisine. This was not unusual for the time; the hot food offered by global competitors of the era was characteristic of their home country, for example, in the 1930s Britain's Imperial Airways' signature dish was the English roast dinner, and it did not incorporate local cuisines, despite its many African and Asian stopovers.[4] Similarly, Pan Am's historic first around-the-world flight of 1947 stands as the quintessential example of airborne cuisine propagating national triumph: the thirteen-day flight featured only 'typically American' dishes such as beef steak, deep fried potato balls and ice cream tart.[5]

Pan Am may have brought American culinary culture to the world, but at first the company did not want to reciprocate, assimilate or even appropriate anything foreign, sticking to reliable American fare. For example, Pan Am claimed credit for the 'first American hamburger joint in Africa', in 1942, following the opening of its wartime Africa-Orient route. The brainchild of executive Santos Ceyanas, the café served beer with hamburgers and was located near Khartoum at the junction of the Blue and White Nile. It was a good example of how Pan Am's food service masked American chauvinism beneath the language of the civilizing mission – its employees were not merely workers, they were – as proudly proclaimed by company propaganda, 'colonizers in the cause of aviation'.[6] The

---

[2] Presland, 'The system of the flying clippers', 33.
[3] Ellyn, '160 mile airline meals good to the last mile'.
[4] Foss, *Food in the Air and Space*, 37.
[5] Van Vleck, *Empire of the Air*, 210.
[6] 'China: Background', University of Miami special collections, Pan Am collection no. 341, series I, box 61, folder 7.

hamburger joint employed a local baker, but instead of incorporating local breads he was instead instructed in how to produce American-style hamburger rolls; likewise, a local butcher was recruited but instructed only to provide the ground meat needed for the burgers. In many ways, the venture provided a pre-echo of the global ascent of the McDonald's franchise. The alcohol was flown in via Pan Am and, as a company history recalls, 'the joint had benches, tables and chairs. It was jammed most of the time. The British patronized the joint too, eager for a view of this output of Yankee civilization.' Hamburgers provided home comfort for flight crews unwilling to eat what the company described as the 'bad food' offered in local 'hell holes'.[7]

Such language was typical of the terminology used to deride local cuisines at the time. This early mistrust of local fare was articulated around scientific concerns about food safety, especially sanitary standards in cities on eastern and African routes, as detailed earlier. The inadvisability of drinking tap water was yet another factor underlying the rise of Coca Cola as a beverage consumed by crew, passengers and locals alike. 'Safe' American food, therefore, acted to neutralize what were essentially imperial exchanges. In 1945 the company's Donald Ranney, an 'old African hand', prepared a detailed thirty-six-page booklet for Pan Am staff who were relocating to its base in Liberia, which contained pages of information on West African history, geography, customs, folklore, politics and everyday life and advice on healthcare and habits while stationed there. Unlike other material of the time, the booklet struck an enlightened tone, cautioning that Liberians were neither 'savages' nor 'niggers' and should be treated with due respect to local traditions and behavioural norms. And yet, remarkably, this extensive summary of Liberia made no mention of local food, instead assuming – of course – that all employees would eat the homogeneous food prepared by company chefs within the Pan Am compound (Figure 5.1). The possibility of consuming local food was simply not contemplated at the time.[8]

Similarly, Pan Am's *Africa News Letter*, produced by and for employees during the war years, listed the dishes cooked by staff stationed in West Africa. It listed the speciality of one Frank Pelikan, 'a motherly sort of fellow', as Irish stew; Fritz Eberhardt and Walter Pelubniak made 'the best ice cream anywhere'; Bill Mitchell made cheeseburgers; and Leland Roke baked cherry pie. For young people away from home, some for the first time, the preparation of such comforting and

---

[7] 'The Cannonball: A history of America's Africa-Orient air lifeline', University of Miami special collections, Pan Am collection no. 341, series I, box 18, folder 7.

[8] 'A handbook for Pan American employees going to Fisherman's Lake, Liberia', c.1945, University of Miami digital collections, Pan Am material.

ELVIRA MURRAY 1947   PHOTO BY W.R. PETERS
                                      PAN AM CO-PILOT

Figure 5.1 Pan Am stewardess Elvira Murray models 'Coca Colonization' in the 1940s. Courtesy: University of Miami Library Special Collections.

familiar food is understandable. Yet all of the cooking took place firmly within the confines of the American base. These salutes to home food favourites were accompanied by a pronounced note of caution about the consumption of local food. It was reported that gazelle meat, caught during hunting trips, was later eaten by some employees but only after first being converted into a standard

European dish and served 'English style, minced with green peas, in a pie'. Any food prepared by locals was definitely not to be trusted, as the *Africa News Letter* went on to explain:

> Pop Feaster and Bill Wersen were off on a special job in the desert several months ago – ran short of meat and shot a gazelle. A local cook fried it according to their instructions but, hungry as they were, it tasted a little odd. The boys asked the cook to show them the shortening he had used. He pointed to a can of lard – but they discovered that its top had not yet been pried off. Next to it, the almost identically shaped can of mosquito cream showed signs of recent use.[9]

In the initial decades of its operation, then, Pan Am functioned – to quote its bluntly titled 'Indoctrination Manual' for employees – as a force bringing 'trade, commerce and advanced civilization to the far corners of the earth'. Its 'founding fathers' – Trippe and Lindbergh – still 'guided the destiny' of the company and its employees as it 'penetrated' new 'virgin territories'.[10] This was the company's self-image from the top-down, for even at executive level culinary tastes in the 1940s remained decidedly American as well. For example, a special 1943 menu for the celebratory dinner marking the inauguration of the international air service between New Orleans and Latin America was stoutly North American in flavour. Latin American dignitaries, various state and federal officials, and Juan and Betty Trippe sat down to a meal of half broiled milk-fed chicken, hash browns and green peas and butter followed by ice cream. Remarkably, given the occasion and location, neither the dinner menu nor the food contained more than the barest of hints of French or Spanish.[11] Melville Stone, the executive who authored the otherwise forward-looking memo of 1946 on improving frozen airline meals, encapsulated company thought at the time, arguing that the majority of passengers, who were American, favoured 'good, plain, wholesome things like steak, turkey, chicken, ham' over anything too exotic – 'sweet breads, frogs' legs, and the like' – which were popular only among people, he wrote, who were 'pretending' to be 'gourmets'.[12]

---

[9] Africa newsletter, vol. I, no. 14, 15 October 1942, University of Miami digital collections, Pan Am material.

[10] Atlantic Division Indoctrination Manual, *c.*1945, University of Miami digital collections, Pan Am material.

[11] Menu for dinner to commemorate the inauguration of the international air service, 12 June 1943. University of Miami special collections, Pan Am collection no. 341, series I, box 64, folder 6.

[12] Melville Stone memorandum, 5 December 1946, University of Miami digital collections, Pan Am material. Courtesy of Gabrielle Williams.

The Cold War civilizational mission and the growth of transnational cuisine

It would take the very different geopolitical backdrop of the Cold War for Pan Am's cuisine to decisively shift from the stars and stripes to an embrace of the transnational. Convinced of the transformative possibilities of air travel, Juan Trippe downplayed Cold War anxieties, and in an oft-quoted address to the 1955 annual meeting of the International Air Transport Association (IATA) claimed that 'mass travel by air may prove to be more significant to world destiny than the atom bomb. For there can be no atom bomb potentially more powerful than the air tourist, charged with curiosity, enthusiasm and good will, who can roam the four corners of the world, meeting in friendship and understanding the people of other nations and races.'[13] This was nonetheless a speech delivered from the presumption of American world leadership. Trippe, like other Cold War-era Americanists, did not view American global hegemony as oppressive; rather, the United States was the 'nation of nations'. The Bretton–Woods conference of 1944 had established a post-war international system in which US-controlled institutions like the World Bank, the International Monetary Fund and the General Agreement on Tariffs and Trade would occupy a decisive role in the global economy, later realized through the expansionist liberal capitalism of the Marshall Plan, which guaranteed access to European markets for American products.[14] At around the same time, the first evidence of tentative steps towards embracing new and exotic cuisines appeared. It had been taken at executive level: at one meeting the company's sales managers negotiated, many for the first time, Latin American cuisine consisting of soup à la Dominicana, salad Mexicana, Guatemalan olives, Venezuelan potatoes and Puerto Rican coffee.[15]

With the subsequent globalization of markets, Pan Am's restrictively American culinary bent started to shift. The 1950s witnessed the introduction of the President Special menu and the influence of French gastronomy through the partnership with Maxim's, as outlined previously, with the company increasingly looking to foreign culinary experts. Under Catering Superintendent Kurt Knuessi, the originator of the President Special menu, local produce was

[13] 'The Pan American Story', 1958. University of Miami special collections, Pan Am collection no. 341, series I, box 62, folder 2.
[14] Donald Pease, 'Re-mapping the transnational turn', in Winifred Fluck, Donald E. Pease and John Carlos Rowe (eds), *Re-Framing the Transnational Turn in American Studies* (Dartmouth: DCP, 2011), 1–46.
[15] Van Vleck, *Empire of the Air*, 75.

accorded primacy. Knuessi ensured the best of local produce made it into his creations: Angus beef from Scotland, Kobe beef from Japan, black pearls (caviar) of the Caspian and Pré Salé lamb from Normandy or New Zealand. The emphasis on the local-as-global was made explicit in a 1958 brochure outlining how food tied in with the company's fabled 'system'. Above the caption 'France' was a photograph of fresh vegetables being loaded into a Maxim's catering van and a smiling girl picking orange blossoms, while 'Italy' featured a diligent old cellar-keeper tending to his wines.[16]

In contrast to the American flavour of the 1943 menu mentioned above, by the time of the partnership with Maxim's in 1952, Pan Am's menus had fully embraced the Gallic. A few years later, the menu for the inaugural Stratocruiser flight from New York to Beirut featured mostly French dishes – its main was Caneton Bigarade, Petits Pois Pistolets and Pommes Duchesse. A 1959 special menu devised for the team behind that most quintessential of American television programmes, the Ed Sullivan Show, on the occasion of a special 1959 trip to Moscow, was entirely in French, its centrepiece a choice between the ever-popular Côte de Boeuf and Canard aux Pêches.[17] While French cuisine remained the staple of Pan Am's menus, individual menus were devised for special occasions. For instance the Irish government's 'An Tóstal' festival of the 1950s (an attempt to drum up tourism to Ireland from the Irish-American diaspora, which was supported by the company) was honoured with a menu offering concoctions such as 'Irish Potatoes', 'Emerald Asparagus', 'Green Salad' and 'Gaelic Tart'.[18] Even in the later years of cost-cutting, Pan Am's food service was still tailored to different destinations. Cheeses provide a good example. Flying to Spain, a Manchego cheese was usually served, whereas for France crew served a number of aged cheeses such as St. André and Roquefort. On return trips from England, scones (a small biscuit-like cake) with clotted cream and jam were always served with a nice 'cuppa' tea; for trips to Japan, beef tongue was served; flights to and from Germany were enlivened with rippchen (cured pork cutlets) and sauerkraut (fermented cabbage), an economy dish so popular that very few customers ordered the first-class food option on that route.[19]

There was a clear transition, then, between the solidly American fare of the early years and the later cosmopolitanism of these menus, suggestive of the

---

[16] 'Pan American World Airways System: A story of people, opportunities and services', University of Miami special collections, Pan Am collection no. 341, series I, box 62, folder 2.

[17] Inaugural Stratocruiser menu and Ed Sullivan Show – Moscow 1959 – special menu, Pan Am collection no. 341, series I, box 497, folder 8.

[18] An Tóstal menu, Pan Am collection no. 341, series I, box 497, folder 9.

[19] Interview with Debbi Fuller, 11 January 2018.

emerging cultural battleground of the Cold War era. Despite increased post-war competition, Pan Am continued to be the dominant carrier between the United States and the world. As such, it increasingly offered a transnational cuisine. As detailed, the general standard and eclecticism of airline cuisine was on an upward trajectory, underpinned by greater scientific understanding. Yet geopolitics were also part of the equation. The transnationalism of Pan Am not only offered a lively and multicultural contrast to the relatively drab cuisine of its rival superpower airline Aeroflot, whose New York–Moscow route it competed against from 1968 onwards, it also aimed to reduce the clout of international competition, whether established or new. In 1949 75 per cent of all traffic between the United States and other nations was run by American operators (chiefly Pan Am), but by 1957 this share had fallen to 63 per cent. Under the global system in which bilateral agreements established international air routes, Western European carriers (BOAC, KLM, Air France and Alitalia) still provided the main competition, but a small amount of market share was now occupied by Mexican, Latin American and Asian carriers. There were also small but notable government-subsidized airlines emerging from countries newly independent of colonial rule, such as Air Jamaica and Air India, with the latter commencing flights to New York in 1960. Significantly, many of these carriers offered distinctively indigenous, non-European menus.[20]

Pan Am may have enjoyed political favour, but it did not attract the same government subsidies that some of its international competitors did; the company was therefore forced to box clever, accentuating premium service as a way of protecting its market share. Central to this service was the cultivation of the 'nation of nations' ideal: the food on offer was international and it was served by staff recruited internationally. As the large airlines of the former colonial powers – like KLM and Air France – faced up to the new international competition, so did Pan Am, but whereas the new mood of postcolonialism prompted European carriers to agonize over whether or not the display of national flags on their aircraft's tails was offensive and thus damaging to market share, the airline of the 'nation of nations' – with its distinctive universal blue globe symbol – did not face the same problems. Despite its status as an arm of US imperialism, Pan Am continued to see itself as a benign alternative to European colonialism; in the 1950s it repeatedly warned the US government against allowing British, French and Dutch competition to use 'island colonies'

---

[20] See Martin P. Staniland, *Government Birds* (Lanham, MD: Rowman and Littlefield, 2003), 120–30.

in the Western hemisphere to 'flood capacity'.[21] Instead, through US government funding aimed at eliminating the threat of communism in countries deemed vulnerable to it, Pan Am provided Cold War technical assistance to national airlines across the Middle and Far East as a way of staunching communist expansion.

In reading Pan Am's changing menus as reflective of broader geopolitical conditions there are some important caveats. The culinary shift was partly the product of internal reorganization. Between 1946 and 1957 Pan Am's three divisions (Pacific – Alaska, Latin American and Atlantic) were responsible for establishing their own catering programmes, each producing their own crockery and cutlery too. It was not until the late 1950s that the President Special service introduced a sort of standardized eclecticism.[22] And despite these changes, some famous guests continued to favour plain American fare. In 1978 King Hussein of Jordan married Lisa Halabi, the daughter of Najeeb Halabi, CEO of Pan American Airways 1969–72, and was a regular customer; King Hussein's culinary tastes, recall flight crew, were decidedly American: he always requested Turkey Tetrazzini and American-style hamburgers.[23] And yet it was precisely because Pan Am operated America's global routes that its menus became decidedly less 'American' than domestic competitors like American Airlines, whose food offerings in the 1970s were typified by its 'Americana Service' which offered passengers 'the table of 1775' complete with the Boston Brisket of Beef, the Chicken New Englander and a 'big hunk of pie' for dessert.[24] By contrast, Pan Am's more adventurous offerings were telling of broader changes in American food consumption. As noted before, in the 1930s the greater availability of refrigeration prompted public health experts, chefs and food writers to herald the American consumer's liberation from 'local food'. What they were referring to by 'local food' was a restrictive and unambitious local diet from consumers' immediate surrounds. However, most Americans did not own a refrigerator at that point and suspicion of foreign fare persisted. By the 1950s, and with America's interventionist role in the world established, most Americans came to own a refrigerator. With food preservable for longer and air transport conveying food quicker, 'local food' was now redefined as highly desirable and exotic. In no small way, Pan Am played a role in the redefinition of the local-as-global/

[21] This example is taken from Douglas Campbell, Pan Am vice president, to Russell B. Adams, State Department, 7 May 1951. Truman Library, Russell B. Adams papers, Panagra-KLM file, box 8.
[22] 'Pan Am Catering Items End of WW II through the 1950s', http://www.everythingpanam.com/1946_-_1960.html (accessed 22 January 2018).
[23] Interview with Cornelis Van Aalst, 6 February 2018.
[24] American Airlines advertisement, 1970. Courtesy of Gabriella Williams.

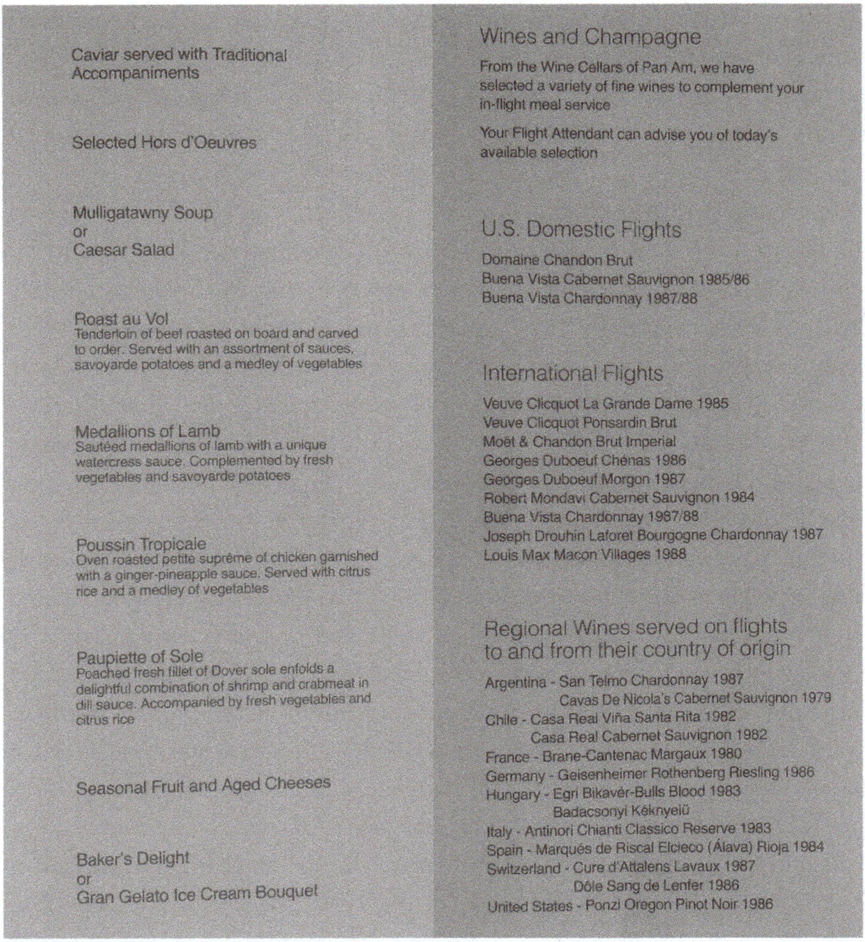

Caviar served with Traditional
Accompaniments

Selected Hors d'Oeuvres

Mulligatawny Soup
or
Caesar Salad

Roast au Vol
Tenderloin of beef roasted on board and carved
to order. Served with an assortment of sauces,
savoyarde potatoes and a medley of vegetables

Medallions of Lamb
Sautéed medallions of lamb with a unique
watercress sauce. Complemented by fresh
vegetables and savoyarde potatoes

Poussin Tropicale
Oven roasted petite suprême of chicken garnished
with a ginger-pineapple sauce. Served with citrus
rice and a medley of vegetables

Paupiette of Sole
Poached fresh fillet of Dover sole enfolds a
delightful combination of shrimp and crabmeat in
dill sauce. Accompanied by fresh vegetables and
citrus rice

Seasonal Fruit and Aged Cheeses

Baker's Delight
or
Gran Gelato Ice Cream Bouquet

Wines and Champagne

From the Wine Cellars of Pan Am, we have
selected a variety of fine wines to complement your
in-flight meal service

Your Flight Attendant can advise you of today's
available selection

U.S. Domestic Flights

Domaine Chandon Brut
Buena Vista Cabernet Sauvignon 1985/86
Buena Vista Chardonnay 1987/88

International Flights

Veuve Clicquot La Grande Dame 1985
Veuve Clicquot Ponsardin Brut
Moët & Chandon Brut Imperial
Georges Duboeuf Chénas 1986
Georges Duboeuf Morgon 1987
Robert Mondavi Cabernet Sauvignon 1984
Buena Vista Chardonnay 1987/88
Joseph Drouhin Laforet Bourgogne Chardonnay 1987
Louis Max Macon Villages 1988

Regional Wines served on flights
to and from their country of origin

Argentina - San Telmo Chardonnay 1987
          Cavas De Nicola's Cabernet Sauvignon 1979
Chile - Casa Real Viña Santa Rita 1982
          Casa Real Cabernet Sauvignon 1982
France - Brane-Cantenac Margaux 1980
Germany - Geisenheimer Rothenberg Riesling 1986
Hungary - Egri Bikavér-Bulls Blood 1983
          Badacsonyi Kéknyelü
Italy - Antinori Chianti Classico Reserve 1983
Spain - Marqués de Riscal Elcieco (Álava) Rioja 1984
Switzerland - Cure d'Attalens Lavaux 1987
          Dôle Sang de Lenfer 1986
United States - Ponzi Oregon Pinot Noir 1986

Figure 5.2 Sample Pan Am first-class menu, late 1980s. Courtesy: Ed Nolan.

global-as-local and this was reflected in its menus. Company publicity from the 1950s claimed to be delivering 'opportunities and new jobs for thousands of people abroad' through its food system.[25] Whereas competitors like Air France and KLM placed emphasis on emblematic national dishes – respectively champagne and camembert, and speculoos and gouda – Pan Am's menus appeared decidedly more internationalist and tailored to specific destinations. The company was becoming a fixture of the Cold War cultural battleground (Figure 5.2).

[25] 'Pan American World Airways System: A story of people, opportunities and services', University of Miami special collections, Pan Am collection no. 341, series I, box 62, folder 2.

Latin American imperial mission

But while the local jobs Pan Am claimed to be creating were indeed built around local produce, they took place under the benign gaze of two presidents – George Washington and Dwight D. Eisenhower – whose faces appear from the clouds in company brochures of the period, two near-celestial overlords overseeing the globalization of taste. Arguably, then, food service provided another example of how the company implicitly suggested that white European-derived norms occupied the highest point in the global cultural hierarchy and that native foods were to be sampled only for white delectation. Ultimately, Pan Am's exotic foods were tailored to national predilections, Western tastes, familiarity and practicality. The supposedly rustic menus in fact owed much to the work of laboratory-based chemical flavourists who, in creating the 'authentic', first assembled the compositions and then carried out the tests.[26] In this way, the transnationalism of airline food lay – not entirely paradoxically – in the increasing uniformity of the global menu.

In examining the broader cultural significance of Pan Am's food service, its much-cited 'system' itself demands scrutiny, and to achieve proper analysis it is necessary to return to the beginnings of the company. The Pan Am 'system' was first mentioned in a shareholders' report of 1933; while the 'system' itself was not defined, it stood for the expansion of the company's brand based around 'visibility assets' and new modern spaces. Food service was of central importance to the 'system' since its materiality – from stewards' dress to the design of menus – reflected the globalizing ambitions of not only the company but also of the United States.[27] With links stemming from Yale and the world of New York finance, links enhanced by his marriage to the daughter of Edward Stettinius, a partner in the corporate finance empire of JP Morgan, the Trippe empire grew alongside the benign attitude of the US State Department. In this era, the dovetailing of the interests of government and big business took place around basic shared views on America's place in the world. Control of sources of raw material and areas for safe investment were the positive priorities, the containment of communism and the exclusion of unwanted products and people

[26] See Jojanneke Claassen, *On the Scent of Taste: The Story of Flavors and Fragrances* (Baarn, Netherlands: Tirion, 1994).

[27] Melissa Aronczyk, *Branding the Nation: The Global Business of National Identity* (Oxford: Oxford University Press, 2013), 30; John Diefenbach, 'The Corporate Identity as the Brand', in John M. Murphy ed., *Branding: A Key Marketing Tool* (Basingstoke: Palgrave Macmillan, 1987), 158, cited in Presland, 'The system of the flying clippers'.

from the United States the negative ones.[28] In the 1920s, 1930s and 1940s, then, Pan Am's monopoly on flights to Latin America was increasingly useful to the US government, not least because it shut out competition from foreign rivals, notably the German carrier Lufthansa. Unlike some other American businesses of the period, the altered political priorities of the 'New Deal' did not dent the company's political favour and its expansion continued apace as more and more Latin and Central American territories were incorporated into Pan Am's system.

Aviation journalist Carl B. Allen would write that Pan Am had proven too tough and large a nut to crack, even for a 'crusading knight in white armor' like President Franklin D. Roosevelt (FDR). After coming to office in 1933, recalled Allen, FDR had condemned the 'fraud and collusion' that had resulted in Pan Am's control of US air services but had come to realize that the network developed by the company was simply too vast to bring under control of the US Army or Navy, and that such a move would have proved 'diplomatically and industrially suicidal'. Allen listed the various branches of the US government that had 'aided and abetted' Pan Am's monstrous growth, a process of 'collusion' that had ensured its status as a 'Yankee national institution in the eyes of our Latin American neighbors'. Despite the whiff of corruption surrounding the airline, Pan Am, wrote Allen, 'has brought 32 Latin American countries and colonies incredibly closer to the United States'.[29]

Consequently, it has been argued that Pan Am played a leading role in constructing the very idea of Latin America, one which was often dismissive and demeaning and based around the colonial notion of exotic subservience.[30] This can be glimpsed through the prism of food. The Fred Astaire movie *Flying Down to Rio* (1933) – which was produced by RKO Pictures in collaboration with Pan Am – symbolized this, featuring scenes in which Brazilian dancers in traditional costume are admired by dining white male protagonists. Foodstuffs would play a key role in this expansion, with Pan Am survey planes identifying suitable sites by dropping large amounts of white flour in areas of jungle or swamp; new air bases were then hacked out by indigenous construction crews, with the workers fed by Pan Am airdrop.[31] If Pan Am's expansion to Latin America in the 1930s

[28] Thomas Cochran, *Business in American Life: A History* (New York: McGraw-Hill, 1972), 161.
[29] Carl B. Allen, 'Malice in Blunderland or the Air Mail Muddle', undated article later published as 'Trouble Aloft!', *New Outlook Magazine* (April 1934). Carl B. Allen papers, box 1, folder 5, WVRAC.
[30] Danielle Mercer, Mariana I. Paludi, Albert J. Mills, Jean Helms Mills, 'Images of the "other": Pan American Airways, Americanism, and the idea of Latin America', *International Journal of Cross-Cultural Management* 17, 3 (2017), 327–43. See also Walter Mignolo, *The Idea of Latin America* (Malden, MA: Blackwell, 2005).
[31] Rosalie Schwartz, *Flying Down to Rio: Hollywood, Tourists, and Yankee Clippers* (College Street: Texas A & M University Press, 2004), 244.

displayed some of the negative traits of white exploration, this was reflected in the food service. In contrast to the array of cuisines offered in later years, in these early days food prepared in Miami was stockpiled for Caribbean and Latin American trips since the local fare was regarded as all but 'inedible'.[32]

Food aid and food security

At the same time, the company performed an important role in aiding food security in the continent. During the 1930s the company bought up a number of Latin American airlines, expanding its size and position. As it did so, it became a source of humanitarian aid at times of natural emergencies, providing food, vitamins and medical supplies to underdeveloped areas of the continent. Carl B. Allen, who embarked on a 15,000-mile round-South America trip courtesy of Pan Am in 1933, described how the company had established thirty-eight weather-watching stations across the Caribbean. After a hurricane had hit the Dominican Republic, killing two thousand people, it was a Pan Am plane which first reached the city and radioed back the dire need of food relief. Allen quoted the president of the country, the authoritarian Rafael Trujillo, as calling the effect of the plane's appearance in the sky as 'miraculous upon our people ... "The plane! The plane!" they cried in a frenzy of new hope. "Now the world knows our terrible plight, help will come." Allen concluded that Pan Am was 'doing much to erase the Latin American suspicion that Yankee interest is always synonymous with Yankee exploitation'. He also noted that Pan Am pilots on Latin American routes would regularly drop parcels containing cookies and candy over particularly 'uncivilized' regions such as the Brazilian jungle in an effort to ensure the goodwill of the locals.[33]

Visiting Panama with Pan Am, Allen observed how 'Yankee sanitation methods have banished flies and mosquitoes, turning a former pest-hole of filth and fever into an earthly paradise'. There were limits to the American civilizing mission, he noted, writing 'several times Uncle Sam has tried to establish model dairy farms in the Canal Zone only to have the most pedigreed and productive cows, after a few months in the tropics, fall to a par in their milk flow with native scrub stock'. Allen also recorded that attempts to establish poultry farms in

---

[32] Pan Am steward Joey Carrera, cited in Helen McLaughlin, *Footsteps in the Sky: An Informal Review of US Airline in-flight Service, 1920s to the Present* (New York: State of the Art, 1994).
[33] Carl B. Allen, Latin American notes, Carl B. Allen papers, box 3, folder 1, WVRAC.

Panama had been unsuccessful, but elsewhere Pan Am's efforts to boost poultry production fared better. Chicken – the principal meat in the staple diet of most countries south of the United States – had been popularized in the Americas by the conquistadores of the sixteenth century, but stock levels and quality had gradually declined over the centuries. In 1929, on a trip south, one of Pan Am's first pilots was disappointed at the quality of chicken served locally and when back in Texas convinced poultry farmers of the potential of exporting hatching eggs south. The first consignment reached Guatemala with only two of 144 eggs broken, signalling the start of a new export trade; the transport of live chicks began when US exporters realized that chicks weighed less than eggs, meaning significant savings on cost. This led, in the 1930s, to a succession of central American governments ordering large consignments through Pan Am in order to improve their national chicken stock. According to a company account 'soon a thousand baby chicks a week were moving down the airways through Central America … the chicks chirped lustily through the days, seemed to relish the flying. And at night one of our station attendants would take them out "for a stretch", change their water, and sprinkle some corn meal on the floor for them.' Soon, the trade had expanded to Latin America with large regular exports to Rio de Janeiro (Brazil) and Lima (Perú) as well as the Caribbean.[34]

Such food transport was in line with the stated priorities of Roosevelt's 'Good Neighbor' policy, namely that trade that enhanced food security be reciprocal, and supplies were flown in the other direction, too. For example, in the 1930s and 1940s Florida's sugar cane crop was repeatedly threatened by plagues of insects. To combat the parasites and save the sugar cane crop, Pan Am – at the request of the US Sugar Company – transported huge quantities of toads native to northern Argentina to Miami. Thanks to the new air routes, fruits native to Latin America but highly perishable – such as papayas, mangoes and passion fruit – increasingly came to be seen on the American plate. Argentine grapes or Chilean melons, which previously arrived less than fresh to American consumers, were now available, more palatable and fresher. The revolutionary potential to the American palate was captured by an interview with a Brazilian food exporter, featured in a company propaganda piece of 1945, who averred that his grandfather 'never would have thought of trying to send fruit specialties to you in the United States. Ships then were too slow. Neither would my father, even after the introduction of steamships. But today I deliver my grapefruit and

---

[34] 'The Flying Clippers of the Southern Americas' (1945), Pan Am collection no. 341, series I, box 64, folder 6.

coconuts to the airport. In less than a day they will be on grocers' shelves in your country.'[35]

Agent of US cultural chauvinism

For all its good, however, Pan Am's expansion also carried with it an occasionally patronizing and imperialistic spirit, as witnessed similarly in its growth in the Pacific. The language used to describe the company's pioneer work in Alaska recurred when it came to the Caribbean, which was likewise described as a 'laboratory' in company literature.[36] The language of the 'laboratory' directly echoed that of the US State Department which, when it came to Latin America, was keen to link technical assistance and cultural relations. The State Department had formally recognized the value of cultural propaganda as foreign policy by creating a Division of Cultural Relations in 1939 and an assistant secretary of state for Public and Cultural Affairs in 1944.[37] The latter post had been created by US Secretary of State Edward Stettinius Jr., none other than Trippe's brother-in-law. The airplane was central to an upbeat pan Americanism that masked US dominance. Following Charles Lindbergh's solo transatlantic flight in 1927, the achievement was initially embraced as a pan American one. His subsequent celebratory tour across Latin America saw him looked upon not as threatening *gringo* but feted by a succession of Latin American leaders as a pioneer who had demonstrated the collective strength and endeavour of the Americas. A year later Trippe, whose company had just been awarded lucrative airmail routes which retraced Lindbergh's 'circle', wrote to him to express his gratitude.[38] This was a harbinger of things to come; although Trippe's airline was named Pan American, it would act as an agent of US expansionism, an airborne extension of the Monroe Doctrine and an opponent to Latin American governments wishing to develop their own airlines. Sugar-coating this fact, in 1929 Trippe dispatched the universally popular Lindbergh and his new wife, Anne Morrow Lindbergh (daughter of US ambassador to Mexico, Dwight Morrow) on a goodwill tour of the continent, where they were wined and dined extensively.[39] But a company

[35] 'The Flying Clippers of the Southern Americas' (1945), Pan Am collection no. 341, series I, box 64, folder 6.
[36] 'History of Pan American World Airways' (1946), University of Miami special collections, Pan Am collection no. 341, series I, box 196, folder 10.
[37] Hart, *Empire of Ideas*, 3.
[38] Van Vleck, *Empire of the Air*, 53–64.
[39] Van Vleck, *Empire of the Air*, 71.

history of 1942 all but spelled out the fact that the company's pan Americanism would actually connote white Americanism; it drew positive comparison between its work in opening up Latin American routes and that of 'the bloody conquistadores driving their conquests through virgin land with sword and flame' and 'the hardy pioneers of both Americas slashing their settlements out of the wilderness'.[40] Often, company memos frankly categorized the Latin American nations by their exploitable resources (Brazil: coffee, bananas; Peru: cocoa, sugar, bananas) while lobbying Washington against allowing national governments to develop rival routes.[41]

In the process, far from the elevating and universalist pan American ideal, locals were demeaned. One company press release, from 1958, claimed that the company's first Pacific flights were witnessed by 'islanders who had never seen or heard of an airplane, who were soon to marvel at the huge droning birds passing overhead'.[42] Another scoffed that Latin Americans treated airports as picnic spots, eating food together as they sat and marvelled at the American technology above them.[43] Carl B. Allen, on his round-South America journey in 1933 aboard a Pan Am Clipper, described mountain sides in Haiti 'that still echo to the beat of voodoo drums' and being unable to discern whether lights visible in the distance were signal flares or 'the open air blazes on which the natives cook their food'. On landing, wrote Allen, a Haitian 'peasant woman', her arms 'characteristically, hanging empty at her sides', approached the plane nervously, addressing it as 'avion'; in the marketplaces the natives, 'bare footed or primitively sandaled', bartered away over foodstuffs; the whole place was 'amazingly primitive'.[44] In Cayenne, Allen enjoyed champagne with dinner while watching 'a native dance, a sort of hoochi-koochi, participated in only by negroes and half-caste whites'. In Havana, he availed of 'a generous punch bowl and great stacks of sandwiches dispensed by smiling ladies' while a 'native band' made a 'pantomime' of trying to play the Star-Spangled Banner.[45] In behaviour typical of a privileged white man of his era, Allen avoided local fare wherever possible, opting instead to dine in the air with the Clipper captain on 'cold baked beans, potted ham, crackers, peanut butter and cookies'.[46]

---

[40] 'Story of the East ('Mother') Division, Pan Am collection no. 341, series I, box 64, folder 8.
[41] Memo on Transportes Aereos Militares, Truman Library, Russell B. Adams papers, Peruvian International Airways file, box 8.
[42] 'The Pan American Story', 1958. University of Miami special collections, Pan Am collection no. 341, series I, box 62, folder 2.
[43] Van Vleck, *Empire of the Air*, 74.
[44] Carl B. Allen, Latin American notes, Carl B. Allen papers, box 3, folder 1, WVRAC.
[45] Carl B. Allen, Notes on Havana, undated, Carl B. Allen papers, box 8, folder 7, WVRAC.
[46] Carl B. Allen, Latin American notes, Carl B. Allen papers, box 3, folder 1, WVRAC.

It has been argued that Pan Am's Hawaiian promotional material from the 1940s to the 1960s, which featured images of scantily clad hula girls dancing in front of palm trees, reinforced a white male gaze and an essentially supremacist colonial narrative,[47] an impression that inspection of the relevant archival material relating to food does little to dispel. The diaries of Betty Trippe illuminate the culinary experiences underpinning such corporate orientalism. Writing of her first trip to Hawaii in 1934 with husband Juan she describes a feast thrown in his honour where 'the food was marvellous – octopus, crab, pig, salmon – except for poi, a native dish of some kind of root that tasted like blotting paper. There followed steamed fish, sweet potatoes, chicken, freshly cut sugar cane, soft coconut custard and, lastly, the marvellous pineapple that is grown here.' The dinner finished with suitably 'native' entertainments – 'Hawaiian girls in grass skirts danced the hula' as red and white leis of flowers were placed around the Americans guests' necks.[48]

Encouraging its employees to view themselves as the spearhead of culinary globalization, company propaganda pieces sought to ramp up the cultural challenges that flight attendants had to contend with when it came to food service. 'Pan Am stewardesses have seen confused passengers dump salt and pepper into the coffee and complain about the terrible coffee, and dump salad into the consommé and complain about the horrid consommé,' one began. This was followed by tales (possibly apocryphal) gathered from crew, such as the story of thirty Portuguese agricultural labourers migrating to Venezuela who were utterly mystified by the breakfast cereal served aboard the flight. After stabbing the milk containers and cornflake boxes with knives, spraying the contents all over the cabin, they were alleged to have finally eaten the flakes like potato chips and drank the milk separately. Then there was the story (almost certainly apocryphal) of a passenger wishing to fly to Puerto Rico from New York who boarded a transatlantic flight by mistake. Noticing that she had an extra passenger, as the flight progressed the flight attendant repeatedly checked names, passing by the errant passenger who emphatically repeated his name – Martinez – to her several times and erroneously received several martinis from the flustered attendant as a result.[49]

---

[47] Iris Aya-Laemmerhirt, "Trying to recapture the front": A transnational perspective on Hawaii in R. Kikuo Johnson's *Night Fisher*, in Shane Denson, Christina Meyer and Daniel Stein (eds), *Transnational Perspectives on Graphic Narratives: Comics at the Crossroads* (London: Bloomsbury, 2013), 83–94.

[48] Trippe, *The Diary and Letters*, 54.

[49] 'Life of a Pan Am stewardess – then and now' (undated), University of Miami special collections, Pan Am collection no. 341, series I, box 292, folder 5.

It was hardly surprising that such an imperialist attitude emerged. Through the global ascent of the airplane, Americans were encouraged to 'look down' on the rest of the world, both literally and metaphorically.[50] Dispensing with the liberal language of the age and his erstwhile non-interventionism, Pan Am adviser Charles Lindbergh could write in 1948 that 'for Americans the doctrine of universal equality is a doctrine of death … the existence of mankind depends on American leadership'.[51] It was an attitude underlying the elite patronage networks that enabled Juan Trippe's company to grow. Like many of his connections, Trippe's friendship with Henry Luce – the media mogul whose vision of an 'American Century' based on 'American internationalism' Pan Am aspired to – was the product of their undergraduate days together at Yale. Similarly, President Roosevelt's special wartime envoy to Europe Averell Harriman, who, during the war, advised British Prime Minister Winston Churchill on how he might avail of Pan Am to feed troops in the North African combat zone, was a friend of Trippe's and a fellow Yale man whose investment in Pan Am back in the 1927 had helped to get the company off the ground. Trippe was also close to another Yale graduate, Harry Stimson, Roosevelt's secretary of war, who is said to have helped to overcome FDR's private dislike of the Pan Am founder.[52] These men came from an elite college network; they felt that they had been bred for power, both national and international, and they were now exercising that right, along the way teaching their fellow Americans how to do likewise. Emergent consequently was an unequal process of global trade liberalization, favouring American agribusiness and securing US dominance.

The 'chosen instrument' and the Cold War

After the Second World War, the US government considered the expansion of the airline industry to be vital to its economic growth both nationally and internationally[53] and, against the backdrop of the unfolding Cold War, Pan Am's bids to further extend routes – to the Far East, the Middle East and

---

[50] Van Vleck, *Empire of the Air*, 95.
[51] Charles Lindbergh, *Of Flight and Life* (New York: Scribner, 1948), 38.
[52] Matthew Brady, 'War Plan Juan: The strategy of Juan Trippe in Latin America and Africa before and during World War II' (unpublished thesis, School of Advanced Air and Space Studies, Maxwell Air Base, Alabama, 2012).
[53] See Civil Aeronautics Administration, *Civil Aviation and the National Economy* (Washington, DC: US Department of Commerce, September 1945), Truman Library, Harry S. Truman papers, official files, box 30, OF 3-H.

Latin America – would be 'favorably considered' by the Harry S. Truman administration.[54] At the same time, Pan Am's status as the 'chosen instrument' of the US government began to be chipped away at. Its subsidies from the government for carrying mail were reduced in 1953, a sign of growing competition for international routes and the gradual waning of official patronage.[55] The extent of the company's political influence raised eyebrows: in 1952, for example, Pan Am found itself under investigation by the Civil Aeronautics Board (CAB) for attempts to curry favour with influential people by offering free flights featuring lavish food.[56] It was an open secret, for example, that Maine Senator Owen Brewster received such favours and, accordingly, led the fight on Capitol Hill for Pan Am to remain the 'chosen instrument'.[57] Yet even as competition in the airline industry intensified and Pan Am's 'complete monopoly' and 'chosen instrument' status was challenged, the CAB noted that company continued to enjoy all the 'advantages' of being 'first in the field'.[58] As a leading American brand and a powerful symbol of US-spearheaded globalization, it remained well regarded by Washington. After all, Pan Am had positioned itself in the vanguard of America's global advance. Previously it had proved a bulwark against German expansion in Latin America and Japanese expansion in the Pacific and now, as the Cold War took hold, against the Soviet challenge. For although domestic political pressure was mounting against 'a billion-dollar government subsidized "chosen instrument" monopolizing American participation in international transport', so too – looking east – was the perceived Soviet threat.[59] And as Trippe testified when called before the president's Air Policy Commission in 1947, Aeroflot, like the majority of the other 'foreign flag competition', was a monopoly 'supported financially at home and diplomatically abroad by their respective governments'.[60]

---

[54] Memo on 'Route Allocations to Permit Pan American Airways to Provide Competitive Service' (1945, undated, unsigned), Truman Library, Harry S. Truman papers, official files, box 30, OF 3-I.

[55] 'Facts and Figures – 1955', University of Miami special collections, Pan Am collection no. 341, series I, box 62, folder 7.

[56] Donald Nyrop, 'Report on civil Aviation June 1951 through October 1952', Truman Library, Harry S. Truman papers, official files, box 31, OF 3-I.

[57] Oral History Interview with George P. Baker, Truman Library, Oral History collection.

[58] Civil Aeronautics Board, Memo for the President, 'Latin American Airlines Case', Truman Library, Harry S. Truman papers, official files, box 38, OF 3-I.

[59] Correspondence between Senator Pat McCarran and Carleton Putnam (Chicago and Southern Airlines); C. C. Campbell, 'Soviets Bidding for Big Air Role', *Barron's National Business and Financial Weekly*, 17 July 1944. Truman Library, George C. Neal papers, International Aviation file, box 18-4.

[60] Statement of Juan Trippe before the president's Air Policy Commission, Washington DC, 1 October 1947. Truman Library, Records of the President's Air Policy Commission, Pan American Airways System file, box 9.

In the opening stages of the Cold War, Dean Acheson, US secretary of state under Truman and a key architect of foreign policy in the period, remarked that 'there's no politics in food'.[61] As Acheson knew, that is untrue. American aircraft would play a major role in transporting food into the narrow confines of Tempelhof airport in the West German capital during the Berlin Airlift of 1948–9, thus reducing the success of the Soviet blockade. Tracy Voorhees, President Truman's adviser on food, had convinced the president that 'the Germans had to be fed, not too much, but they had to have enough to live'.[62] By the spring of 1949, daily tonnage arriving in Berlin by air was approaching 9,000 tons, most of it food and medicine, and most of it delivered by American Overseas Airlines (A.O.A.), which was soon incorporated into Pan Am.[63] Such endeavours became the stuff of legend and, although always formally acting as an individual agent, Pan Am continued to facilitate the growth of US might. Juan Trippe maintained that Pan Am carried 'cargoes of goodwill' not 'cargoes of imperialism and hate'; as the historian Jenifer Van Vleck notes, through such statements corporate Americanists like Trippe were able to bolster the material infrastructure of empire while simultaneously sustaining a cultural denial of imperialism.[64]

The company's relationship with the US government may have been tested by periodic economic challenges, but it continued to be mutually beneficial.[65] In 1950, in a landmark victory against competitor airline TWA, the US government awarded Pan Am the routes of its one other Atlantic rival, A.O.A., ensuring Pan Am possessed the greatest market share on European routes until the 1970s. According to Truman's administrative assistant Stephen Spingarn, this decision was the result of skulduggery: both the Civil Aeronautics Board and the president had decided that TWA should win the contract but, later, 'the White House telephoned and asked that the file be returned ... the President's signature was erased clumsily, then added to a memo disapproving the decision'. Consequently, Pan Am retained 'the lion's share of the pie'.[66] Other reports alleged the use of 'an ink eradicator and also an eraser' in what came to be known as 'the case of the missing signature'.[67] For Pan Am, it clearly paid to have friends in

[61] Oral History Interview with Stanley Andrews, Truman Library, Oral History collection.
[62] Oral History Interview with General William H. Draper, Truman Library, Oral History collection.
[63] Pan Am Historical Foundation, 'The Big Lift', https://www.panam.org/pan-am-stories/546-the-big-lift (accessed 25 September 2018).
[64] Van Vleck, *Empire of the Air*, 128.
[65] Erik Benson, 'The chosen instrument? Reconsidering the early relationship between Pan American Airways and the US Government', *Essays in Economic and Business History* 22, 1 (2014), 97–110.
[66] Oral History Interview with Stephen Spingarn, Truman Library, Oral History collection.
[67] 'CAB opens original Truman order for examination', Truman Library, Russell B. Adams papers, Daily Diary 1950, file 5, box 28.

high places. Later, the company continued to service the US military in conflicts such as Korea and Vietnam and received the majority of its charter contracts until the mid-1960s. During the latter conflict, the company's flight attendants regularly volunteered to carry out 'morale boosting' visits to wounded soldiers at the Da Nang base in Vietnam and, as part of a major 'milk and ice cream plan', brought dairy products – a much-appreciated taste of home – to injured soldiers in military hospitals.[68]

More broadly, the food of Pan Am, like the company itself, operated as an 'instrument' of US soft power. One of the most famous Cold War exchanges around food occurred in 1959, with the so-called 'Kitchen Debates' between Soviet Premier Nikita Khrushchev and US Vice President Richard Nixon at the opening of the American national exhibition in Moscow. Part of this 'cultural exchange' was the construction of a suburban house, complete with housewife and various domestic labour-saving devices. In the kitchen of the model house Nixon, who had flown to Russia with Pan Am, proudly pointed to the ease with which the average American housewife could go about food preparation thanks to superior American technology, to which Khrushchev sarcastically asked if the Americans had also devised a machine that 'puts food into the mouth and pushes it down'.[69] This, the quintessential Cold War diplomatic incident involving food, might well have been complemented by another, involving Pan Am's meal service. A former Pan Am employee recalled Khrushchev's arrival in New York one year later on the occasion of the 902nd Plenary Meeting of the United Nations General Assembly in 1960, during which the Soviet premier infamously removed his shoe and banged it on the desk. Pan Am was tasked with servicing Khrushchev's plane for the trip, removing its galley equipment and reprovisioning it for the flight to Russia. While being cleaned in the Pan Am kitchens at Idlewild Airport, New York, the Russian plastic ware – unable to withstand the high temperatures of the latest American dishwashers – melted into indistinguishable plastic blobs. Although this might well have provided the United States with a potential propaganda coup, the incident was not reported; Pan Am employees quickly and discretely replaced all the Russian ware with Pan Am dinnerware, thus avoiding any kind of international incident (Figure 5.3).[70]

---

[68] *Wing Tips*, vol. 1, no. 10, November 1967, University of Miami digital collections, Pan Am material.

[69] See Ruth Schwartz Cowan, *More Work for Mother: The Ironies of Household Technologies* (New York: Basic Books, 1983).

[70] Phillip Parrott, cited in Whyte, 'The early pursers: Chief cooks, bottlewashers, and in-flight typists'.

Figure 5.3 Transporting Food Bounties to the World, Pan Am promotional material, 1960s. Courtesy: University of Miami Library Special Collections.

Orientalist expectations

From its inception, Pan Am took its place in what one historian has described as a nexus of 'corporate capitalists and a powerful artistic, intellectual and political Anglo elite' for whom a streamlined and aerodynamic 'conformity of body and machine' informed by racial hierarchies would ensure social and aesthetic stability.[71] The Second World War challenged such presumptions and during the Cold War Pan Am touted its stewardess corps as a 'Junior League of Nations'. It came under increasing criticism in the 1950s, however, for hiring white foreign employees while at the same time refusing to hire African American flight attendants. Defending the policy, the company cited the discrimination such members of staff would face in destinations such as Bermuda and South Africa, where colour bars operated.[72] According to one

---

[71] Cogdell, 'The futurama recontextualized: Norman Bel Geddes's eugenic "world of tomorrow"', 242.
[72] *New York Amsterdam News*, 10 March 1956. University of Miami special collections, Pan Am collection no. 341, series II, box 308, folder 6.

history, Pan Am's solitary employment of black staff up to this point was Trippe's personal team of African American manservants who kept him and his family fed and watered in his Washington, DC, townhouse, and occasionally the local labour casually contracted to help with cargoes and provisioning at exotic destinations.[73] In early airline posters advertising the food available at different locations 'natives' were depicted as just that – scantily clad, lithe yet backward, a source of entertainment but always separate from the advanced Europeans and their technology. Accordingly, when consuming food on America's established international carrier, many passengers expected exotic entertainment, even after the company's hiring policy shifted. One of Pan Am's African American flight attendants, who flew its Caribbean routes and spoke the requisite Spanish, recalled an exchange during meal service in the 1970s with a white female passenger who remarked, 'My goodness, your English is so nice! My husband thinks you're from Jamaica, but I bet you're from Trinidad.' Their faces dropped in disappointment when she revealed she was from Philadelphia.[74]

Perhaps inevitably, some of this orientalism inevitably crept into meal service. In the 1950s and 1960s the company over-hired Japanese-American and Japanese women in an attempt to draw customers away from Japan Airlines. In company literature describing food service, these flight attendants were distinguished from their colleagues as 'diminutive' and 'soft-spoken'.[75] This reinforced the image of the food server as an alluring, exotic subservient geisha, with the company boasting how experiencing service from a woman of 'oriental ancestry' would allow passengers to 'taste the charm of the Orient'.[76] This exoticism was laid on thick on flights to and from Japan, right down to the ornate chrysanthemums decorating the menus.[77] A special company feature on the first cohort of Japanese-born flight attendants training in Miami claimed 'they have discovered you can't beat hamburgers and ice cream' and 'rice is no problem because American southerners love rice, too'. The orientalist narrative continued, boasting of how 'girls who have never cooked much besides sukiyaki will learn to prepare and serve a seven-course gourmet dinner with Maxim's of Paris flair'; the climax came with the description of the distinctive food service offered by

---

[73] Bender and Altschul, *The Chosen Instrument*, 366.

[74] Barry, *Femininity in Flight*, 119.

[75] 'First Japanese Girls trained as Pan American stewardesses' (1966), University of Miami special collections, Pan Am collection no. 341, series I, box 292, folder 6.

[76] Vantoch, *The Jet Sex*, 109. Elsewhere, it is argued that part and parcel of the notion of the 'Pan Am family' were the restrictions placed on non-white staff. See Kenneth Hudson and Jennifer Pettifer, *Diamonds in the Sky: A Social History of Air Travel* (London: Bodley Head, 1979), 22.

[77] Reiko Yano, *Airborne Dreams*, 29, 69.

these Japanese women, one marked by 'culinary arts and social graces'.[78] Pan Am was not alone in this: as a means of advertising the fact that it offered an Asian service, in the 1950s Northwest Airlines ramped up the orientalism, naming the cocktail lounge on its Stratocruisers the Fujiyama Room and decorating the plane with bonsai trees and Japanese symbols.[79]

Overall, it is apparent that Pan Am under-recruited flight attendants from recently decolonized countries in places such as Africa, the Middle East, the West Indies and non-Japanese Asia relative to European, North American and Japanese staff. Neither was there any comparable effort to include cuisine from these postcolonial regions in menus (apart from the very occasional embrace of Middle Eastern dishes). Instead, the company's menus reflected the same sort of limited diversity that distinguished its recruitment, with flights to different nations in Europe marked by distinct menus, while the same diversity of choice did not tend to occur in flights to countries from the decolonizing world.

An unmistakably orientalist tone was struck in a gushing gastronomic salute of 1977 entitled 'You Are Where You Eat', which was commissioned for the airline's fiftieth anniversary and published in the in-flight magazine *Clipper*. It repeated many of the exoticizing staples around food that typified the company's earlier years. Commencing with a quote from German writer Johann Wolfgang von Goethe misattributed to the great British naval explorer Captain Cook – 'when a man eats the fruit of more favored climes he is for the moment transported thither, and imagination heightens the enjoyment' – the article went on to list the culinary delights the author had witnessed thanks to Pan Am. These included 'a young boy tenderizing an octopus by pounding it into the beach' in Tahiti; 'a belly dancer undulating all that Allah gave to her' in Istanbul while the writer consumed a kebab; and market stalls in Mexico where the turtle was 'fit for a Mayan king'.[80] Similarly, the priority for Pan Am's transnational troupe to entertain in the course of food service was illustrated in 1981 with the hiring of renowned Chinese classical singer-dancer-actor Yu Lu. Lu, the headline recruit for Pan Am's new China route, was a star of stage and screen, often cast in roles which involved him dressing up in the elegant attire of ancient China. In an interview he stated 'doing a delicate balancing act in the aisles of a jet with a tray full of meals and drinks has a lot in common with

[78] 'First Japanese Girls trained as Pan American stewardesses' (1966), University of Miami special collections, Pan Am collection no. 341, series I, box 292, folder 6.
[79] Foss, *Food in the Air and Space*, 85.
[80] Robert L. Sammons, 'You are where you eat', *Clipper* (July 1977), 67–74.

whirling, wheeling and pirouetting on stage in a traditional Mandarin sword dance'.[81]

Attention to detail

And yet beneath the tall tales and chauvinism lay a genuine attention to culinary choice and authenticity which underpinned the airline's leading global position. The company actively sought customer suggestions on how to tailor its menus towards tastes distinctive to certain flight routes because of the typical type of passenger on them. For example, a large volume of German passengers flying from Europe to Argentina requested Al'Ancienne (coarse grain) mustard to go with their beef; this duly became standard on all Buenos Aires flights in 1988.[82] Pan Am's consistent attention to detail stands in contrast to what one historian calls the 'faux multiculturalism' of the meal service on other American carriers. For example, Northwestern Airlines' multi-course 'Regal Imperial' service featured – as part of a messy amalgam of cuisines – Scandinavian pastries, followed by shrimp in Indian currie (sic) sauce, frankfurters in 'customized' sauce, lobster tail with duchess potatoes, Italian white wine, champagne (from New York) and 'fancy after-dinner mints'. Pan Am also remained aloof when confronted with the gimmickier efforts of its transatlantic competitors, like TWA in the 1960s, which checked passengers' passport details prior to departure so that they could offer a complimentary layer cake to anyone whose birthday it was. The same company's 'Foreign Accent Service' featured flight attendants serving English, French or Italian food in disposable paper costumes: respectively, a barmaid's dress, a French gown and a Roman toga.[83] Pan Am's staff, by contrast, were genuinely – and unsleazily – international.

When it came to provisioning, staff were encouraged to use their initiative if a demographic predominated on a particular flight. If it was known that a flight would contain a large number of teenage exchange students, for example, it was up to the purser to order more soft drinks for that particular flight.[84] A former flight attendant remembered that, when she was young, her father had a business

---

[81] Yu Lu clipping, University of Miami special collections, Pan Am collection no. 341, series I, box 379, folder 7.

[82] Pan Am Monthly operational bulletin, vol. 18, no. 7, August 1988, University of Miami digital collections, Pan Am material.

[83] Foss, *Food in the Air and Space*, 99.

[84] Pan Am Monthly operational bulletin, vol. 16, no. 11, October 1986, University of Miami digital collections, Pan Am material.

trip to Rio de Janeiro and took the family. They flew Pan Am, the return trip falling on a Friday. When the menus were passed out she saw that they offered a choice of entrées, one of which was fish. Knowing there would be a great many people of the Catholic faith on the plane, and thus that Friday fish would be a popular choice, the company had included a disclaimer in small print in the menu footer: 'Should fish no longer be available, Juan Trippe has received special dispensation from the Pope for other entrées to be selected.'[85] It was almost as if Trippe, master of the skies, was equal in status to God's representative on earth.

Underlining the capitalist virtue of choice, by the 1960s Pan Am were offering special menus with a choice of diabetic, Kosher, salt-free, vegetarian and Hindu options.[86] Occasionally, these increased options led to unexpected difficulties. For example, the company was surprised by the high number of passengers requesting Kosher meals on its Puerto Rico service – despite there being very few people of the Jewish faith taking this flight route. The reason was that the 'ordinary' meal at that time chiefly consisted of sandwiches whereas the Kosher option was a full hot meal.[87] In later decades, in a spirit of equality, both hot or cold meal options had to be provided to meet religious differences in consumption and greater attention was paid to the detail of religious beliefs governing the consumption of food. In 1989, following queries from Jewish passengers about whether the ware in which food was served was unglazed earthenware (and thus Kosher-able) the airline reassured them that the flatware and china provisioned with Kosher meal choice had never been used and were acceptable under Kosher law.[88]

The opening up of the airline market in the same decade also brought with it a change in the passenger demographic, bringing with it renewed consideration of dietary habits informed by people's sociocultural background. The company noted that most people were now flying economy, even business travellers were opting for the cheaper option; and, increasingly, there was a marked increase in 'passengers visiting friends and relatives', adding '(mainly ethnic)'.[89] Accordingly, menus were adjusted. New regional specialty menus were designed for First Class, with chicken and lamb curries served with raita and pickles for flights to the Indian subcontinent. Although the company prided itself on using local

---

[85] Interview with Susan Taylor Davis, 31 January 2018.
[86] Lynn Homan and Thomas Reilly, *Images of Aviation: Pan Am* (Stroud: Arcadia, 2000), 115.
[87] Foss, *Food in the Air and Space*, 126.
[88] Pan Am Monthly operational bulletin, no. 4, Fourth Quarter, 1989, University of Miami digital collections, Pan Am material.
[89] Pan Am Monthly operational bulletin, vol. 18, no. 6, July 1988, University of Miami digital collections, Pan Am material.

expertise and local ingredients, the speciality meals were not necessarily those of the country where a flight originated; the Indian meals, for example, were provisioned from the company's kitchens in London, where ingredients for Indian dishes were more readily available.[90] To properly accommodate Hindu passengers, the company issued circulars containing information emphasizing how Hindu dietary laws prohibit the consumption of pork and beef alongside a glossary of different Indian dishes.[91]

By the 1980s, the amount of dietary restrictions and requirements among customers had increased considerably. In 1969, following the White House Conference on Food, Nutrition and Health convened by President Richard Nixon, US regulation shifted away from controlling food composition and towards more extensive labelling which provided consumers with more information on the product they were eating, including ingredients, additives and fortifications. Consumers were becoming more informed about what exactly constituted the food they ate. Symptomatic both of increased consumer concerns about healthy diets and the marketability of healthy foods was the 1978 legislation regulating the proper labelling of foodstuffs claiming to be 'reduced calorie' and 'low calorie'.[92] At the same time, consumers were baffled by extensive labelling which listed additives, leading to the common lament about the garbage infesting modern food and the quest for food purity. By 1985 Pan Am was noting that the number of 'nutrition-conscious passengers' had increased across all classes of service and therefore introduced more cold items on light fare menus such as pasta and vegetable salads served with duck, tuna, chicken and crab meat and continental breakfast options such as yoghurt, fresh fruit and pastries.[93]

The company now had to design its menus to meet the dietary requirements of vegetarians, vegans, pescatarians and customers with allergies of different varieties. Customers who ordered a special meal (for instance, diabetic or low sodium) were required to receive the same type of meal (hot or cold) as the other passengers. Crew were also increasingly aware of the health implications of food choices. The company's in-house bulletins increasingly contained suggestions from staff like the following: 'where a cold snack is served, would it be possible to change the menu to something which is not full of fat and preservatives? I feel

---

[90] Pan Am Monthly operational bulletin, vol. 15, no. 3, August 1985, University of Miami digital collections, Pan Am material.
[91] Pan Am Monthly operational bulletin, vol. 16, no. 13, December 1986, University of Miami digital collections, Pan Am material.
[92] Junod, 'Food Standards in the United States', 184.
[93] Pan Am Monthly operational bulletin, vol. 15, no. 3, August 1985, University of Miami digital collections, Pan Am material.

our passengers would be happier and healthier.'[94] Given the consumption of food by flight staff and anxiety over weight checks, the subtext to this request may have been concerns about the impact of in-flight food on the flight attendant's own diet and weight. The company responded to this particular suggestion by adding fruit to the snack rotation cycle.

The mounting imperative of economy

The expansion of choice around healthier foods was obscuring a more pressing incentive, however. Quite simply, in the competitive airline marketplace of the 1970s and 1980s there was also a strong financial incentive to offering high-fibre and low-cholesterol food: it was much cheaper.[95] From 1974, what were internally known as 'thrift' trays were used in economy class, housing 'healthier' food items which were now smaller in size.[96] In the same year, the company's management estimated the cost saving from using smaller salt and pepper sachets alone to be $147,000 per year.[97] This reflection on smaller salt and pepper sachets provides a pre-echo of one of the most famous management case studies, the case referred to as Crandall's Olive. In the 1980s Robert Crandall, head of American Airlines, is widely reputed to have come up with an ingenious cost-cutting measure after contemplating his salad. Picking up the olive on top of his leaves he reasoned that the removal of this single item would not be noticed by passengers and could save his airline a lot of money. The humble olive was, accordingly, removed from American Airlines' salads. Reputedly, the implementation of this small economy measure saved the company $40,000 a year.[98]

The familiar theme of financial expediency would also limit aspects of choice for Pan Am's customers in the 1980s. The company's extensive menus spoke to the blending of capitalism and democracy and the juxtaposing of capitalist choice with communist austerity. This was an integral theme of the West's propaganda campaign throughout the Cold War, encapsulated in President Ronald Reagan's famous put-down of Fidel Castro in 1983 when he

---

[94] Pan Am Monthly operational bulletin, vol. 18, no. 7, August 1988, University of Miami digital collections, Pan Am material.

[95] Susan Timper, 'Catering to customer expectations', *Clipper* (November 1990), 4.

[96] Pan Am Monthly operational bulletin, vol. 18, no. 6, July 1988, University of Miami Libraries digital collections, Pan Am material.

[97] Pan Am Monthly operational bulletin, vol. 46, December 1974, University of Miami digital collections, Pan Am material.

[98] Andrew Serwer, 'Business penny-pinching adds up', *ABC News*, 23 May 2001.

imagined a Cuban crowd clamouring for American snack foods and chanting 'peanuts! popcorn! crackerjacks!'. Yet Coca Cola, integral in Pan Am's delivery of American foodstuffs to the world, was off the menu on many routes in the late 1980s. The post-war global popularity of Coca Cola has been memorably termed 'Coca Colonization'[99] and this de-coupling of America's two most recognizable brands resulted in an upsurge in passenger complaints. The company's director of beverage product selection responded by informing staff 'Pan Am has signed a three year deal with Pepsi-Co to offer only their products and as the agreement is *financially beneficial* to Pan Am, you are asked to democratically advise passengers that our beverage provisioning offers only Pepsi products'.[100]

The disassociation of Pan Am and Coca Cola, the two quintessential American brands, was a sign of the hard times ahead for the airline. Yet former Pan Am employees often describe their shock at the death of the airline in 1991, and in some, the sense of disbelief is still palpable, for how could such an American institution be allowed to collapse? The sense of surprise surrounding Pan Am's demise was sharpened by the widely held notion that the company had done the state some service, particularly in time of war. This notion was itself tied to the idea of the company as a transnational entity: Pan Am was emblematic of a US-led, globalizing, civilizational mission; its staff comprised their very own United Nations; and its range of menus showcased exotic yet accessible food cultures, with the increasing diversity of menus and dietary requirements symbolic of capitalist choice over communist conformity.

The rot, however, had set in long before. Trippe retired in 1968, a year which not only marked the beginning of the end of the airline he founded but also the beginning of the end of the public's romance with air travel. In the same year, President Lyndon B. Johnson marked a departure from the upbeat globalism of the preceding twenty-five years by criticizing US citizens for travelling abroad; instead they should spend their dollars at home in an effort to reduce the balance of payments crisis. Later that year, the travel editor of *Esquire* magazine, who had been a passenger on Pan Am's inaugural jet flight, contrasted the old days of flying – which featured 'a drink or two' and a 'leisurely meal' – with the new experience of cultural homogenization or, as he called it, the 'resort-industrial complex' of mass, cheap travel. Trippe's vision of popular tourism was a victim of its own success, he implied, with tourist spots characterized by 'monstrous

---

[99] See Reinhold Wagnleitner, *Coca-Colonization and the Cold War* (Chapel Hill: University of North Carolina Press, 1994).

[100] Pan Am Monthly operational bulletin, vol. 17, no. 9, July 1987, University of Miami Libraries digital collections, Pan Am material.

buildings' and the sameness of 'hamburger joints and pizza parlors'.[101] Perhaps, despite the Old World pretensions of Pan Am, the industrially processed, standardized frozen meal of William Maxson had won out after all, as symbolized in the rise of the 'TV Dinner' and a homogenizing fast-food culture. The pan American ideal, it seemed, had degenerated into exactly what it was supposedly fighting the Cold War against: a drab uniformity.

For the first time, Pan Am began to experience loss years due to a combination of increased competition, excess capacity on the 747 and recession. In the 1970s the company sought a return to profitability through pursuing economies and cutting jobs but was hit hard by the 1973/1974 world oil crisis. The embargo on oil supplies by the OPEC group of oil-supplying nations placed airlines in dire financial straits and the 'oil shock' formed the backdrop to the US government's Airline Deregulation Act of 1978. Following this legislation, new promotions and marketing experiments ushered in cheaper flights for consumers and giants like Pan Am struggled to cope with carriers which achieved much lower costs through dispensing with catering altogether. The Pan Am-owned Intercontinental Hotels were among the first assets to be sold when the company commenced its long demise in the 1980s, and the hotel chain brought in 500 million dollars when sold in 1981.[102] 'Pan Am's cupboard is almost bare' remarked *Forbes* magazine in 1989, following the sell-off of its vast Pacific network to United Airlines in 1986 and the bombing of Pan Am flight 103 over Lockerbie, Scotland, in December 1988.

The changing nature of the airline market in the 1970s and 1980s had its impact on food service, too, making Pan Am appear increasingly anachronistic. The decline in airline food service in general was flagged by *Economy Traveler* magazine in 1978, which asked why food service was so 'over-emphasized and over-promoted'. The article was symbolic of a new era in which consumer choice and competition would expand and standards fall. 'Simply serving up to 400 people any sort of hot meal under flight conditions is a technological marvel', it conceded, but claimed that economy class airline food was only 'as appetizing as a meal that can be purchased for five dollars at a Howard Johnson's, Denny's or Sizzler Steak House'. Why, then, *Economy Traveler* wondered, did airlines push this aspect of service so? 'A cheap way to score a few points' it concluded,

---

[101] Van Vleck, *Empire of the Air*, 271.
[102] Tatiana Pouschine, 'Pan Am's cupboard is almost bare', *Forbes*, 25 December 1989. University of Miami special collections, Pan Am collection no. 341, series I, box 61, folder 7.

recommending that passengers switch to extra-saving no-meals flights operated by Continental Airlines and competitors.[103]

To Pan Am, which operated international flights and prided itself on the quality, eclecticism and longevity of its food service, such advice may have seemed ignorant and irrelevant. And yet, in the decade to come, the airline's catering department would bear the brunt of the company's panicked economy drive. The 1980s brought significant labour disputes between the company and its catering staff. Deregulation had ushered in a general decline in working conditions and Pan Am's final decade would be marked by industrial clashes which eroded the loyalty and goodwill built up among employees over years. After faring poorly for several years, in 1984 the company sought to remove a guarantee against lay-offs within its catering division agreed with the Transport Workers Union in 1980. This led to strike action by catering employees which only ended in 1985 when the company agreed to keep on just 75 of its 750 catering employees. Pan Am's great sell-off of its once-proud in-house catering facilities was already underway; the Marriott Corporation was brought in to provide catering services instead and, by 1987, the sell-off of all in-house catering services was complete, leading to a lawsuit by the remaining in-house staff who found themselves redundant.[104]

The company's deteriorating fortunes saw it acquire National Airlines in 1981, a move resented by Pan Am's flight attendants who thought that National's flight attendants lacked the training and gravitas they possessed. 'They are the hot dogs and we are the caviar' was a common put-down. Pan Am staff, after all, did not view themselves as mere 'waitresses in the sky' but rather the crème de la crème of international service professionals.[105] The company tried to wrestle with these tensions, acknowledging the challenges of deregulation but urging staff to ensure Pan Am was more competitive by attention to 'value-added': 'that extra glass of water half way through the movie'.[106] As the Cold War wound towards an end, the company continued to function as an informal instrument of US soft power through food. In 1990 the company gained publicity for its 'Candy Clipper', a 747 laden with chocolate for Romanian children suffering amidst the country's political upheaval following the ousting of dictator Nicolae Ceaușescu. The

[103] 'Selecting a Domestic Airline Flight', *Economy Traveler*, vol. III, no. I (February 1978), University of Miami special collections, Pan Am collection no. 341, series I, box 306, folder 18.
[104] *Daily Appelate Report*, 23 September 1987. University of Miami special collections, Pan Am collection no. 341, series I, box 61, folder 7.
[105] Ana Lacombe, interviewed 15 March 2018.
[106] Pan Am Monthly operational bulletin, vol. 18, issue 6, July 1988, University of Miami digital collections, Pan Am material.

big-bellied 747 allowed more room for the transport of commercial cargo, often vegetables and fruit imported from Latin America. The 'Candy Clipper', on the other hand, was the brainchild of Pan Am mechanic Jeff Musheno, who resolved on the project after hearing that chocolate had been decried as a 'capitalistic evil' by the previous regime and that many Romanian children had consequently never tasted it. The company reported that 'the Romanian military state police welcomed Jeff as the truckload of chocolate wound its way through the cities and towns of Romania. As they entered town after town they were greeted with cheers of "Pan Am" and "Chocolate!"'[107] There are shades of the Berlin Airlift, and even the Liberation of Europe, to the story of the 'Candy Clipper', with malnourished Europeans gratefully receiving 'the sweet taste of freedom', but these were fainter shades. Pointedly, the triumph of the United States in the Cold War would coincide with the folding of its 'chosen instrument'; arguably, too, the demise of Soviet communism meant that Pan Am's operations, and not least its cultural capital, were no longer as valuable to the US government as they once had been. The opening up of the airline industry had demonstrated that Pan Am was no longer the sole, or even leading, carrier of an American version of the 'good life'. Alternative agents of American cultural diplomacy had emerged, alternative and more efficient globalizing forces.[108]

---

[107] 'Jeff Musheno and the Candy Clipper: The sweet taste of freedom', *Clipper*, April 1990, 6.
[108] See Rob Kroes, 'American empire and cultural imperialism: A view from the receiving end', *Diplomatic History* 99, 23, 3 (1999), 463–78.

Conclusion

The brainchild of Juan Trippe, Pan Am and its global 'system' was based around the creation of a unified luxury experience which placed both the company and the United States at the forefront of modernity.[1] When Pan Am's China Clipper completed the first Pacific crossing by air in 1935, the company took its place in the annals of global circumnavigation, its executives and pilots imagining themselves as latter-day Magellans or Columbuses (indeed, one of its early Caribbean Clipper fleet was named 'Christopher Columbus'). The company became a transnational phenomenon: the latest example of how transoceanic communication and exchange functions as a major motor of transformation in history.[2] Central to this global system, as this book has demonstrated, was the carrier's food service. In an attempt to mimic the ocean liner experience, the notion of luxury dining in the air had long been a dream of the industry's visionaries. It was attempted aboard the airships and later, as aircraft took over, the notion of the airplane-as-hotel/restaurant emerged. Yet technological constraints militated against these designs. It would take the technological progress wrought by the Second World War and the subsequent jet age to transform the possibilities, both literal and metaphorical, of high dining; Pan Am was perfectly placed to realize these, coming to occupy a vanguard position in the soft power contest of the Cold War.

By the end of the Cold War, though, it is hard to escape the conclusion that Pan Am's usefulness to the US government had expired and, with it, the cultural and political will to sustain its operations had disappeared. By 1991 the airline and its famously transnational food service would be firmly consigned to the realms of nostalgia. Theorists of global 'food regimes' identify a first period c.1870–1914 during which European powers were dominant; a second 'regime'

---

[1] See Presland, 'The system of the flying clippers'.
[2] See Rainer F. Buschmann, *Oceans in World History* (New York: McGraw-Hill, 2007).

*c.*1945–1970s associated with American hegemony; and a latter period during which global trade became freer. If we are to follow these conceptualizations, Pan Am was chiefly an engine for the second 'food regime', having laid much of the groundwork for it in the 1920s and 1930s. This was a period during which food aid, trade and cultural propaganda dovetailed with US strategic aims, US-led technological progress and US-dominated institutions, bolstering the United States' image and securing the loyalty of foreign states.[3] But after the oil and food shocks of the 1970s, a more intense global trade liberalization arose in the 1980s, one in which the 'chosen instrument' lost its air of exclusivity and in which it was no longer the principal agent of the pan American ideal.

The strange afterlife of the world's greatest airline

Such is the lingering appeal of the Pan Am brand that in 1998, following its collapse seven years earlier, the company's curious afterlife began. It was bought out of bankruptcy by Pan Am Systems, a company which briefly operated Pan Am flights along the US East Coast. Pan Am Systems' air operations ceased in 2004 but it was the business backer behind the 2011 'Pan Am' television show. A second revival occurred in 2016 when Pan American World Airways – an exclusive jet service – began operating private charters across the United States. An affiliated company, Pan Am Brands, sells expensive replicas of the distinctive blue Pan Am bag which, in the 1960s, was given to first-class passengers and celebrities at check-in and signified the privileged lifestyle of the international jet set.[4]

The international glamour of Pan Am's food service, however, can never be fully revived. That does not stop former employees from trying. The quality of Pan Am's food offerings is still looked upon with pride by former employees today, most of whom are in their senior years. During research for this book, I was invited to the Miami home of a former flight attendant who recreated the first-class dining experience for me and six other guests, all of whom were former company employees. With the help of a retired purser, and with both octogenarians dressed in their old Pan Am uniforms, they served up what was – without exaggeration – an epicurean feast. The eight-course dinner featured an

---

[3] André Magnan, 'Food', in Helmut K. Anheier and Mark Juergensmeyer (eds), *Encyclopedia of Global Studies* (New York: Sage, 2012).
[4] https://panambrands.com/ (accessed 23 August 2018).

array of dishes and liquors, free-flowing wine, exemplary service and stimulating conversation. Original Pan Am first-class menus adorned the table: the iconic silver-blue menu of the 1970s featuring an ample wine and champagne list and a mouth-watering choice of mains – roast tenderloin of beef, sautéed medallions of lamb, chicken suprême in ginger-pineapple sauce and poached Dover sole. When I entered the suburban house, I was instructed by my hosts to pretend instead that I was entering a plane and was even given a genuine flight ticket to present after 'pre-departure' drinks and before I was shown onto 'the plane' and to my seat. The cutlery and crockery bore the company logo and the plates depicted the Clippers of yore. On visiting the bathroom, I noticed that there were original toothpicks and hand towels which were embossed, too, with the distinctive company logo.

As this story shows, when Pan Am folded, many employees not only took with them their uniforms and other paraphernalia, they took cherished memories of their working lives as well, and – arguably – a heavily nostalgized ideal of US global hegemony. Accordingly, many are keen to maintain an idealized image of the company they loved and after dinner one fellow guest fretted at how frank some of her former colleagues had been in disclosing some of the hidden aspects of food service. Others are more forthcoming about the unpalatable aspects of working for Pan Am. Nonetheless, nearly all former employees remain united in their admiration for the company's founder (still referred to, reverently, as 'Mister Trippe'); their disdain for what they view as the over-sexed image of Pan Am in contemporary culture; and a nostalgia for the high standards of food service during the 'golden age' of airline dining and US power.

Exporting the pan American ideal

The nostalgia is understandable. Through its food service, Pan Am played a key role in making American national symbols (such as the imperial eagle adorning the President Special glassware) into international icons. It also provided a means of exporting American consumer culture abroad, most notably through its association with brands like Coca Cola and Heinz, heralding capitalist colour over communist uniformity. At the state dinner thrown by President Richard Nixon to honour the Apollo XI astronauts in 1969, the now veteran aviation journalist Carl B. Allen found himself sitting next to Clare Booth-Luce, the wife of Henry Luce, the media baron who had originally coined the term 'American Century'. Both recalled a journey they had taken thirty-eight years previously in 1931 in a 'flying bath tub' – a rickety prototype 'flivver plane' – when Booth-Luce was editor of *Vanity Fair*, a trip which ended in a crash landing.[5] America had just conquered the moon and Allen, sitting in the White House, marvelled at how far his nation had progressed, progress achieved over the space of a mere generation, in securing international dominance and now beyond, into the final frontier. The United States had gone from flying bathtubs to space shuttles.

Yet American power in the twentieth century went beyond the purely technological, it established the transnational. Pan Am's food service stood for a hierarchy of taste cultures that was inherent to this trend. While anyone in the world could order a Coca Cola, only those at the higher end of the hierarchy could boast of having enjoyed a regional wine specially selected for a flight to its country of origin – such as a Brane-Cantenac Margaux on a flight to Paris – at 45,000 feet. Faithful to Juan Trippe's vision, the company succeeded in collapsing the culinary borders between the New and the Old World. The jet age food culture forged by Pan Am developed in tandem with the US-led globalization of capital and commerce in the second half of the twentieth century. In this brave new world, the oppressive old boundaries of time, space and place were collapsed; as a 1959 Pan Am press release boasted, 'the jet age passenger will eat breakfast in Tokyo and arrive in San Francisco three hours before the meal he just ate.'[6]

Although Pan Am was inherently elitist, Juan Trippe's vision of democratized air travel allowed many more people to buy into this previously restricted vision. Often, entry to this exclusive club amid the clouds was through the medium of food, with economy class passengers enjoying Maxim's branded dishes through the revolutionary introduction of pre-packaged food, frozen in aluminium, then later oven-heated. Moreover, the company would pioneer the majority of scientific innovations around the airborne consumption of food, transforming eating at altitude from an uncomfortable endurance into a more pleasurable experience. From a position of near monopoly, Pan Am made the world a smaller place, in the process globalizing taste, expanding palettes and championing the notion of fresh, locally sourced food. This process was characterized by a divide between modernism and tradition, between the Old World and the New, which – through its culinary offerings – the company attempted to bridge. Trippe's spirit was encompassed in the ideal of the company he founded: the Pan American ideal of progressive transnationalism.

[5] Notes and correspondence with Clare Booth-Luce, September 1969. Carl B. Allen papers, box 9, folder 3, WVRAC.
[6] Van Vleck, *Empire of the Air*, 263.

At the same time, the opening up of the airline industry would expose just how wedded the company was to an elitist – and at times orientalist, archaic and faintly racist – notion of food service and food servers, one whose contradictions were being exposed and increasingly undermined by broader social change and the pursuit of economies. When it came to food, Pan Am's impact went far beyond the cultural: opening up swathes of the planet; aiding food security and delivering food aid; and – through the transit of foodstuffs – helping to transform the global food system and, with it, the global plate. In doing so, however, it also functioned as an instrument of US imperialism and broader globalization: a process which has also delivered an unhealthy culinary homogeneity. In its pioneering early days, this was evident in the frontier spirit accompanying its quest for new markets and the promise of abundance; in its latter years, against the continuing backdrop of the Cold War, the company came to symbolize American hegemony through a selective culinary transnationalism. At its worst, then, Pan Am can be seen as a leading agent of Coca Colonization or, to put it another way, the globalization of everything.

As the millennium beckoned and the 'American Century' matured, flying increasingly became a business like any other, illustrated most clearly in the deteriorating edibility of airline food, with quantity trumping quality in almost every respect. By the late 1980s, both Pan Am and the US government were over-reached and the airline's death in the early 1990s, coinciding with Western triumph in the Cold War, would mark the end of an era. In 1991 the *Financial Times* reported on a group of youths near a New York subway punching the air as they chanted, 'Pan Am! Pan Am!' – they were greeting the news that the company, which would go on to fold within the year, had been granted temporary permission to keep on operating. Why? Because Pan Am represented 'all that was modern, prosperous and confident about the US'. Thirty years later, the same newspaper was reporting on how the public had fallen out of love with American airlines.[7] Although US globalization would continue apace, its upbeat and progressive mood – symbolized in the culinary transnationalism of its airborne 'United Nations' – would give way to increased global competition and a questioning of America's global role. Although the American dream has persisted into the twenty-first century, by the end of the twentieth century the old pan American ideal – and Pan Am, the airline that propagated it through its food culture – had become a thing of the past.

[7] Michael Skapinker, 'Frequent flyer: How we fell out of love with the airlines', *Financial Times*, 6 April 2020.

Bibliography

Archival collections

British Airways Heritage Centre
Delta Flight Museum Archives
Foynes Flying Boat and Maritime Museum
Georgia State University Archives
Hoover Presidential Library
National Air and Space Museum Archives
Northwest Airlines History Center
Pan Am Historical Foundation
Pan Am Museum Foundation
Science History Institute
The College of Surgeons, Philadelphia
Truman Presidential Library
University of Miami Archives and Special Collections
West Virginia University Regional and Archives Center

Newspapers, periodicals, reference

Aero International
Aerokurier
Air and Space
Airline World
Airliners
Airlines International
Caminos del Aire
Chicago Tribune
Christian Science Monitor
Clipper
The Economist
Economy Traveller
Executive Travel
Financial Times
Flight Global

Flight Magazine
Forbes
Fortune
Harvard Business Review
Huffington Post
Jet Wings
Life Magazine
Los Angeles Times
New Horizons
New York Herald Tribune
New York Lifestyles Magazine
New York Times
The New Yorker
Pan Am Africa News Letter
Pan Am Monthly operational bulletin
Pan Am System Sales Clipper
Pan American Air Ways
Pan American World Airways Teacher
Plane and Pilot
Reuters Aeronautical News
Sabor
Scandinavian Traveller
The Times of London
Time Magazine
Wall Street Journal
Washington Post
Wing Tips
Wings
The Woman Magazine

Books, articles, pamphlets

Albala, Ken. *The Food History Reader: Primary Sources* (New York: Bloomsbury, 2014).
Apple, Rima D. 'Vitamins win the war: Nutrition, commerce, and patriotism in the United States during the Second World War', in David F. Smith and Jim Phillips (eds), *Food, Science, Policy and Regulation in the Twentieth Century* (Abingdon: Routledge, 2000), 135–49.
Aronczyk, Melissa. *Branding the Nation: The Global Business of National Identity* (Oxford: Oxford University Press, 2013).

Banks, George. *Gourmet and Glamor in the Sky: A Life in Airline Catering* (London: GMS, 2006).

Barry, Kathleen. *Femininity in Flight: A History of Flight Attendants* (Durham, NC: Duke University Press, 2007).

Bender, Marylin, and Altschul, Selig. *The Chosen Instrument: Pan Am, Juan Trippe, and the Rise and Fall of an American Entrepreneur* (New York: Simon and Schuster, 1982).

Boothby, E. J., Clark, M. S. and Bargh, J. A. 'Shared experiences are amplified', *Psychological Science* 25 (2014), 2209–16.

Brady, Matthew. 'War plan Juan: The strategy of Juan Trippe in Latin America and Africa before and during World War II' (unpublished thesis, School of Advanced Air and Space Studies, Maxwell Air Base, Alabama, 2012).

Bratt, Aimee. *Glamor and Turbulence – I Remember Pan Am, 1966–91* (New York: Vantage, 1996).

Buschmann, Rainer F. *Oceans in World History* (New York: McGraw-Hill, 2007).

Caron, Francois. 'Un chantier à ouvrir: l'histoire de la restauration à la SNCF. Premières orientations', *Revue d'histoire des chemins de fer* 41 (2010), 227–41.

Claassen, Jojanneke. *On the Scent of Taste: The Story of Flavors and Fragrances* (Baarn, Netherlands: Tirion, 1994).

Cochran, Thomas. *Business in American Life: A History* (New York: McGraw-Hill, 1972).

Cogdell, Christina. 'The Futurama recontextualized: Norman Bel Geddes's eugenic "World of Tomorrow"', *American Quarterly* 52, 2 (2000), 193–245.

Connolly, N. D. B. 'Timely innovations: Planes, trains and the "whites only" economy of a Pan-American city', *Urban History* 36, 2 (2009), 243–61.

Cowan, Ruth Schwartz. *More Work for Mother: The Ironies of Household Technologies* (New York: Basic Books, 1983).

De Syon, Guillaume. 'Is it really better to travel than to arrive? Airline food as a reflection of consumer anxiety', in Lawrence C. Rubin (ed.), *Food for Thought: Essays on Eating and Culture* (Jefferson, NC: McFarland, 2008), 277–93.

De Syon, Guillaume. 'Airmeals: We are what we eat, but what happens when we fly?', *Sabor* 1 (2013), digital issue.

Desgrandchamps, Francois, and Donzel, Catherine. *Cuisine à bord: Les plus beaux voyages gastronomiques* (Paris: Editions de la Martinière, 2011).

Dick, Harold, and Robinson, Douglas. *Golden Age of the Great Passenger Airships* (Washington, DC: Smithsonian Press, 1985).

Douganis, Rigas. *Flying Off Course: The Economics of International Airlines* (London: Routledge, 2010).

Dunning, Eugene. *Voices of My Peers: Clipper Memories* (Nevada City: Clipper Press, 1993).

Edington, Sarah. *The Captain's Table: Life and Dining on the Great Ocean Liners* (London: National Maritime Museum, 2005).

Foss, Richard. *Food in the Air and Space: The Surprising History of Food and Drink in the Skies* (Langham, MD: Rowman and Littlefield, 2014).

Frahm, Harry. *Above and Below the Clouds: Recollections* (Frankfurt: Von Goethe, 2013).

Freidberg, Susanne. *Fresh: A Perishable History* (Cambridge, MA: Belknap, 2009).

Grew, Raymond. *Food in Global History* (Boulder, CO: Westview, 1999).

Hart, Justin. *Empire of Ideas: The Origins of Public Diplomacy and the Transformation of US Foreign Policy* (Oxford: Oxford University Press, 2013).

Hesser, Leon. *The Man Who Fed the World: Nobel Peace Prize Laureate Norman Borlaug and His Battle to End World Hunger* (New York: Park East Press, 2010).

Holmes, Bob. *Flavor: The Science of Our Most Neglected Sense* (New York: W. W. Norton, 2017).

Holmes, Richard. *Falling Upwards: How We Took to the Air* (New York: Random House, 2013).

Homan, Lynn, and Reilly, Thomas. *Images of Aviation: Pan Am* (Stroud: Arcadia, 2000).

Howard, Michael. *Transnationalism: An Introduction* (Jefferson, NC: McFarland, 2011).

Hudson, Kenneth, and Pettifer, Jennifer. *Diamonds in the Sky: A Social History of Air Travel* (London: Bodley Head, 1979).

Hühne, Matthias. *Pan Am History, Design and Identity* (Berlin: Callisto, 2017).

Jarvis, Paul. *British Airways: An Illustrated History* (London: Amberley, 2014).

Junod, Suzanne White. 'Food standards in the United States: The case of the peanut butter and jelly sandwich', in David F. Smith and Jim Phillips (eds), *Food, Science, Policy and Regulation in the Twentieth Century* (Abingdon: Routledge, 2000).

Kaplan, James. *The Airport* (New York: Morrow, 1994).

Kelly, Erby. 'Public Appetite; Dining Out in Nineteenth Century Boston' (unpublished PhD dissertation, Emory University, 2010).

Kriendler, Jeff, and Baldwin, James Patrick. *Pan Am – Personal Tributes to a Global Aviation Pioneer* (Miami: Pan Am Historical Foundation, 2017).

Kroes, Rob. 'American empire and cultural imperialism: A view from the receiving end', *Diplomatic History* 99, 23, 3 (1999), 463–78.

Kurlansky, Mark. *Birdseye: The Adventures of a Curious Man* (New York: Random House, 2012).

Leebaert, Derek. *Grand Improvisation: America Confronts the British Superpower, 1945–1957* (New York: Farrar, Straus and Giroux, 2018).

Levenstein, Harvey. *Paradox of Plenty: A Social History of Eating in Modern America* (Oxford: Oxford University Press, 1993).

Lindbergh, Charles. *Of Flight and Life* (New York: Scribner, 1948).

Luce, Henry. 'The American Century', *Life Magazine*, 7 February 1941.

Magnan, André. 'Food', in Helmut K. Anheier and Mark Juergensmeyer (eds), *Encyclopedia of Global Studies* (New York: Sage, 2012), digital issue.

Mahoney, Lawrence. *The Early Birds: A History of Pan Am's Clipper Ships* (Miami: Pickering Press, 1987).

McCool, Audrey. *Inflight Catering Management* (New York: John Wiley, 1995).

McLaughlin, Helen. *Footsteps in the Sky: An Informal Review of U.S. Airlines Inflight Service 1920s to the Present* (Evanston, IL: State of the Art, 1994).

McLaughlin, Philip, and Tibère, Laurence. 'Tourisme et altérité alimentaire', *Espaces* 202 (2003), 37–47.

Mercer, Danielle, Paludi, Mariana I., Mills, Albert J. and Mills, Jean Helms, 'Images of the "other": Pan American Airways, Americanism, and the idea of Latin America', *International Journal of Cross-Cultural Management* 17, 3 (2017), 327–43.

Mignolo, Walter. *The Idea of Latin America* (Malden, MA: Blackwell, 2005).

Mintz, Sidney. *Sweetness and Power: The Place of Sugar in Modern History* (New York: Penguin, 1986).

Morshed, Adnan. 'The aesthetics of ascension in Norman Bel Geddes's Futurama', *Journal of the Society of Architectural Historians* 63, 1 (2004), 74–99.

Nielsen, Georgia Painter. *From Sky Girl to Flight Attendant: Women and the Making of a Union* (New York: Cornell University Press, 1982).

Parrott, Philip J. *The History of Inflight Food Service* (Houston: International Publishing Company of America, 1986).

Pease, Donald E., and Rowe, John Carlos. *Re-Framing the Transnational Turn in American Studies* (Dartmouth: DCP, 2011).

Pellis, Richard. *Modernist America: Art, Music, Movies, and the Globalization of American Culture* (New Haven, CT: Yale University Press, 2012).

Peterson, Barbara. *Rapid Descent: Deregulation and the Shakeout in the Airlines* (New York: Simon and Schuster, 1994).

Pilcher, Jeffrey. *Food in World History* (New York: Routledge, 2006).

Poulain, Jean Pierre. 'S'adapter au monde ou l'adapter? L'alimentation en mouvement, des grandes migrations au tourisme', *Diasporas, 7 – Cuisines en Partage* (2005), 11–28.

Poulain, Jean Pierre, and Larrose, Gabriel. *Traité d'ingénierie Hôtelière Conception et organisation des hôtels, restaurants et collectivités édition augmentée* (Paris: Editions Jacques Lanore, 1995).

Presland, Tony. 'The system of the flying clippers: Designing Pan American Airways' (unpublished MA dissertation, University of Oxford, 2018).

Rose, Alexander. *Empires of the Sky: Zeppelins, Airplanes, and Two Men's Epic Duel to Rule the World* (New York: Penguin, 2020).

Sandoval-Strauss, A. K. *Hotel: An American History* (New Haven, CT: Yale University Press, 2007).

Sanghvi, Vir. *Rude Food: the Collected Food Writings* (New Delhi: Penguin, 2004).

Scholliers, Peter, and Teughels, Nelleke (eds). *A Taste of Progress: Food at International and World Exhibitions in the Nineteenth and Twentieth Centuries* (Farnham: Ashgate, 2015).

Schwartz, Rosalie. *Flying Down to Rio: Hollywood, Tourists, and Yankee Clippers* (College Street: Texas A & M University Press, 2004).

Sheller, Mimi. *Aluminium Dreams: The Making of Light Modernity* (Cambridge, MA: MIT Press, 2014).

Sheward, Erica. *Aviation Food Safety* (Oxford: Blackwell, 2006).

Shields, David. *The Culinarians: Lives and Careers from the First Age of American Fine Dining* (Chicago: University of Chicago Press, 2017).

Spang, Rebecca. *The Invention of the Restaurant: Paris and Modern Gastronomic Pleasure* (Harvard: Harvard University Press, 2000).

Spence, Charles. 'Tasting in the air: A review', *International Journal of Gastronomy and Food Science* 9 (2017), 10–15.

Staniland, Martin P. *Government Birds* (Lanham, MD: Rowman and Littlefield, 2003).

Strauss, David. *Setting the Table for Julia Child: Gourmet Dining in America, 1934–1961* (Baltimore, MD: Johns Hopkins University Press, 2011).

Sutter, Joe. *747: Creating the World's First Jumbo Jet and Other Adventures from a Life in Aviation* (New York: Smithsonian, 2006).

Tiemeyer, Phil. *Plane Queer: Labor, Sexuality, and AIDS in the History of Male Flight Attendants* (Los Angeles: University of California Press, 2013).

Trautman, James. *Pan American Clipper: the Golden Age of Flying Boats* (Erin, Ontario: Boston Mills, 2007).

Trippe, Betty. *The Diary and Letters of Betty Stettinius Trippe* (McLean, VA: Paladwr: 1982).

Vantoch, Victoria. *The Jet Sex: Airline Stewardesses and the Making of an American Icon* (Philadelphia: University of Pennsylvania Press, 2013).

Van Vleck, Jenifer. *Empire of the Air: Aviation and the American Ascendancy* (Cambridge, MA: Harvard University Press, 2013).

Wagnleitner, Reinhold. *Coca-Colonization and the Cold War* (Chapel Hill: University of North Carolina Press, 1994).

Waldo, Myra. *The Complete Round-the-World Cookbook* (New York: Doubleday, 1954).

Weirather, Larry. *The China Clipper, Pan American Airways and Popular Culture* (Jefferson, NC: McFarland, 2006).

Williams, Susan. *Savory Suppers and Fashionable Feasts: Dining in Victorian America* (New York: Pantheon, 1985).

Williamson, Jefferson. *The American Hotel: An Anecdotal History* (New York: Knopf, 1930).

Williot, Jean-Pierre (ed.). *La restauration ferroviaire entre représentations et consommations* (Frankfurt: Peter Lang, 2017).

Yano, Christine Reiko. *Airborne Dreams: 'Nisei' Stewardesses and Pan American World Airways* (Durham, NC: Duke University Press, 2011).

Zimring, Carl A. *Aluminium Upcycled: Sustainable Design in Historical Perspective* (Baltimore, MD: John Hopkins University Press, 2017).

Index